Hotel Kid

HOTEL TAFT
NEW YORK
SEVENTH AVENUE AT FIFTIETH STREET

HOTEL TAFT
NEW YORK

SEVENTH AVENUE AT FIFTIETH STREET

T0273821

"TARRY AT THE TAFT"

PAUL DRY BOOKS
Philadelphia 2002

Hotel Kid

A Times Square Childhood

by Stephen Lewis

First Paul Dry Books Paperback Edition, *2004*

Paul Dry Books, Inc.
Philadelphia, Pennsylvania
www.pauldrybooks.com

Parts of this book, in somewhat different form,
originally appeared in Gourmet Magazine.

Text type: Galliard
Display type: Futura, Shelley Allegro Script
Composed by P. M. Gordon Associates
Designed by Adrianne Onderdonk Dudden

1 3 5 7 9 8 6 4 2
Printed in the United States of America

Library of Congress Cataloging-in-Publication Data

Lewis, Stephen, *1929*–
Hotel kid : a Times Square childhood / by Stephen Lewis —
1st Paul Dry Books ed.
p. cm.
ISBN *0-9679675-8-9* (hardcover : alk. paper) —
ISBN *1-58988-018-8* (trade paper : alk. paper)
1. Lewis, Stephen, *1929*–Childhood and youth.
2. New York (N.Y.)—Biography.
3. New York (N.Y.)—Social life and customs—*20th* century.
4. Taft (Hotel : New York, N.Y.)—Biography.
5. Hotelkeepers—New York (State)—New York—Biography.
6. Taft (Hotel : New York, N.Y.)—History—*20th* century.
7. Times Square (New York, N.Y.)—History—*20th* century. I. Title.

F128.5 .L694 *2002*
974.7'1043—dc21   *2002004747*

ISBN *1-58988-018-8*

For Harpo

Hotel Kid

arricades in front of the Michelangelo, a small hotel on Manhattan's West Side, force pedestrians and taxis into a narrow stream in the middle of the street. It is a week before the hotel officially opens. Assorted big shots from the Italian hotel chain that owns the hotel are flying in from Milan for the inaugural reception. Workmen are on their knees, troweling tiny imperfections from fresh, wet pavement. Exiting a cab to give my bag to the uniformed doorman, I block a line of cars all the way to Sixth Avenue and set off every horn on the West Side.

Though it is morning, it seems late afternoon. Tall office buildings line the block, cutting off the light. Once, I remember, Fifty-first Street was dappled. The sun rising over the East River shone through the lacework of the Sixth Avenue El. Empty lots lay fallow, waiting for the Depression to end. Rockefeller Center, under construction, was silhouetted in a silver nimbus in the morning; in the evening, it turned gold.

The doorman waits for me on a pathway of narrow boards over the new pavement, balancing with a bag in each hand. Precariously, I follow him into the lobby. Opera from hidden loudspeakers surrounds us: Pavarotti singing "Nessun Dorma"—"No one is sleeping." Not the most apt selection for a hotel. I turn around and around like a dog getting ready to lie down. The newsstand is missing. In fact, I can't orient myself at all until I realize that the hotel entrance has been moved in about ten feet from the street. Then the lobby comes into focus.

To my right, an Italian restaurant has set up shop where the key and mail desk should be. To my left, a storage area has replaced a bank of a dozen pay telephones. Ahead, at the lobby's far end, a beige marble registration desk cuts the room short by twenty feet. The Michelangelo has been built into, onto, and around the old Hotel Taft, a Times Square fixture for fifty years. Little is left of the original structure but the floors and the elevator shafts. The Taft bar, a giant horseshoe to the east of the lobby that sheltered a half dozen bartenders within its curve, is now the lobby of a condominium next door. Half of the lower floors of the old hotel and everything above the tenth floor belong to the condominium. The remainder has been transmuted into this 250-room beige boutique hotel.

The Taft was the biggest hotel in midtown and, until Rockefeller Center went up, the tallest building in the neighborhood. According to millions of matchbook covers and picture postcards, it offered "2000 Rooms With Bath on Times Square and Radio City." Out-of-town couples danced there at lunchtime, and high-school kids on spring break who had never been in an elevator before rode up and down for hours, their eyes rolling wildly, like mustangs'.

I once asked my father, who was general manager of the Taft for thirty-three years, how it was possible to live both at Times Square and at Radio City. I was pleased to have caught him in this rare error, but he patted me on the head and explained that it was advertising. When I grew older, I learned that there never had been 2,000 rooms, either. At the hotel's opening in 1926, the owners announced 1,700 rooms. Later, workmen knocked down walls to combine small rooms into bigger ones. In the 1950s, reporting on one of the many changes in ownership my father endured, the *New York Times* counted 1,437 rooms. At the time of Father's death in 1976, the newspaper, perhaps out of courtesy, brought the count back up to 2,000. Illusion is as necessary to a hotel as a passkey. Growing up, I learned that not everybody who smiles is happy. Not everyone who says "Thank you" is grateful. Not every waiter who dances in pain to your table crying

"Careful, sir, careful. Plate is very hot!" is holding a warm plate.

My brother, Peter, and I grew up at the Taft in a four-room suite at the end of a corridor on the fifteenth floor, overlooking the roof of the Roxy Theater next door. Most of what we know, right and wrong, we learned at the Taft. Much of what we take for granted, other people don't know at all. Before I finished the third grade, I knew what to do with a swizzle stick—though I still see people my age trying to put their eyes out with them. On the other hand, I was forty before I learned what storm windows were for.

We moved to the Taft in 1931. I was eighteen months old and Peter seventeen months younger than that. We ate, slept, got hugged, got spanked, got sick, and got well in rooms 1586, 1587, 1588, and 1589. When we were grown, those four rooms were still our family home—the place where we went to see Mother and Father, bring girl-friends, eat free meals, and stay when we were broke. Our childhood home had more rooms than yours, more maids, and a dance band in the basement. But if you re-turn home after thirty years, there will probably be strangers in the rooms where you grew up, too.

Above the registration desk in this new truncated lobby, I see a wall where the mezzanine should be, a bal-cony lined with heavy bronze doors. One door led to the telephone room, where half a dozen switchboard operators answered and placed calls; another opened to a conference room that doubled for wedding receptions, occasionally tripling for birthday parties—mine. Behind the third door, marked *Private,* young women opened invoices from suppliers and travel agents, letters requesting room reservations, and illiterate, illegible scrawls that invariably turned out to be requests for souvenir matchbooks. In front of a small room with smoked glass panels, Father's secretary joked and flirted with travel agents on the phone while Father, behind the smoked glass, worked without anyone's daring to interrupt him. Anyone with a complaint—or even a compliment—had to make do with an assistant manager. These men sat in a little glass booth in the lobby, in striped trousers and dove-gray jackets. Their title and air of quiet authority were devised to placate angry guests.

"What do you mean my room's not ready? I want to see the manager." "Here's Mr. Robinson, our assistant manager."

"It's after midnight. There's a drunk in the next room. Get me the manager." "Just a minute, sir. I'll connect you with the assistant manager."

"THERE'S A COCKROACH IN THE BATHROOM!" "Oh, sir! I'm so sorry, sir. Here's the assistant manager."

In his daily log, the assistant manager wrote down the problems he had faced on his shift and what he had done to make or keep guests safe and happy. Father read that log intently. Then, half a dozen times a day, he left his office behind the smoked glass panels and walked out past the clerks, suddenly quiet. He'd tour the lobby, the kitchens, and the hotel's three restaurants. Six feet tall, handsome, in a dark blue suit, he moved as stiffly as a leading man in a silent film. He made his rounds walking slowly, hands clasped behind his back, looking straight ahead, missing nothing. When he had circled the restaurant or reached the far end of the lobby, he'd nod to the maitre d' or the bell captain or the assistant manager (watching him anxiously, trying not to show it), who would hurry to his side, leaning toward him like a sunflower toward the sun, to find out what he had spotted in his two-minute walk that everyone else had missed for the entire shift.

From the time Peter and I were old enough to roam the hotel by ourselves, we knew that we were not to run up to him, not even to wave to him when he was on his rounds. Mother explained that he hated to be stopped. He might be distracted and miss a dead lightbulb or a bellman with unshined shoes.

To the left of the registration desk, I see only three elevators instead of the six I grew up with. The three missing cars must be on the other side of the wall, carrying condo owners through their share of my childhood home. The elevator doors are the original Taft doors, burnished bronze and decorated with small relief rosettes. It is unsettling to see them without a crowd waiting to get on. Even with six cars, the Taft elevators were packed. Peter and I used to run back and forth, checking the dials above the doors to see which floor each car was on, trying to guess which would reach the lobby first. That's not as easy to do as it sounds. It isn't always the car in the lead that arrives first; that's the one that makes the most stops picking up passengers on the way down. Sometimes, two cars stop at the same floor at the same time—guests hesitate, make false starts, first to one car, then the other, while a third sails by on its way to the lobby. The ability to guess which elevator will arrive first is a skill Peter and I still have, though we don't find much use for it anymore.

When Mother, returning from a rare visit outside the hotel, walked through the lobby, a ripple of deference flowed in her wake. She was always impatient to get back upstairs. She'd shift her weight from leg to leg, like some exotic heron, while the elevator emptied. As the last passenger exited, she'd get on, nodding to the operator to close the door. If he was new and didn't know her, she would tell him to close the door and go. By then, the starter had seen her; at five foot nine or so and fond of hats with veils, she was hard to miss. He'd walk over, flip his hand upward, the doors would shut, and she'd rise.

When all the elevators were busy on other floors, Mother would nip around to the porter's desk to take one of the service cars there. The men on duty would rise and stub out their cigarettes when she walked through the unmarked bronze door that led to the back. If a new man started to explain to her that the guest elevators were around the corner, the other porters would tell him it was okay. One day, she found out what she should have guessed: that sometimes guests die in their rooms, and when they do, they don't leave in a passenger car. In the service elevator, tapping her foot impatiently, she was riding up to the fifteenth floor when the car stopped and two men entered, pushing a white-sheeted gurney too long to be a room service table. Realizing what it held, she screamed, "Get off! Get off! Are you deaf? Off! Off!"

Children who visit their father's law office or paint factory once a year are momentarily embarrassed at the fuss made over them by the people who work there. Peter and I were fussed over at breakfast, lunch, and dinner, when we went out, when we came back in, when we went downstairs to the newsstand for a candy bar.

When we were old enough for school, we chatted with more than a dozen friends before we left the building. We spoke first with the telephone operator who rang us with a wake-up call. Walking down the corridor, we said hello to the chambermaids. We kidded with the elevator man and greeted the starter and the bellmen. Walking across the lobby, we waved to the lady who sat in a glass booth across from the assistant manager, under a sign that said "Ask Miss Allen." A concierge, though not called that then, she distributed maps and directions, twofers to Broadway plays (tickets that allowed the holder to buy two for the price of one), and free tickets to radio broadcasts at Rockefeller Center. Whoever was hired to sit in the booth was called Miss Allen.

Entering the Taft Coffee Shop, a sunny room with plate glass windows that looked out on Seventh Avenue, we said hello to the hostess, the waitresses, the countermen, and any of Father's staff who might be grabbing an early cup of coffee. We sat at the counter on red leatherette stools and ordered orange juice, eggs, and sometimes pancakes, too. Back in the lobby, after a hello to the assistant manager, the cashiers, the key clerks, and the mail clerks behind the front desk, we stopped to talk with Mr. Greene the Bell Captain—powerfully built, very polished, in unquestioned control of the bellmen and elevator operators—who perched on a high stool behind his own marble podium. We spoke to the couple at the newsstand, and out we went through the revolving door, waving goodbye to the Fifty-first Street doorman, who would tell us to be careful crossing the streets.

When we were older, taking the subway to a different school uptown, we'd go down to the kitchen to pick up our lunches, giant sandwiches in brown paper bags. Then we'd say hello or wave to even more people, otherwise hidden in the basement: kitchen workers grabbing a smoke in the pantry halls, room service waiters, bakers. We greeted everyone we passed—except the bootblack outside the barbershop, who talked to himself in a constant unintelligible monotone. The barbers told us he had been badly wounded in the First World War.

Once I took the wrong subway and found myself lost in Harlem. "Steve!" I turned and saw a Taft bellman across the street. I walked over and asked him which way back to the subway. "I'll take you there," he said. I told him not to bother, just to point me in the right direction. "No bother," he said. We walked to the subway together. As I went down the stairs, I turned back and saw him at the top of the stairs, watching out for me.

Most children begin school knowing the names of one or two occupations: fireman and policeman, generally. They often do not know what their parents do, unless they fight fires or arrest people. At the Taft, people's names were their jobs: Charlie the Steward, Bridie the Maid, Smitty the Grill Room Waiter, George the Room Service Waiter, Paul the Pastry Chef, Martin the Chef, Martin the Porter, and Mr. Greene the Bell Captain, all speaking gently to us in the accents of Germany, France, Greece, Ireland, or Lenox Avenue.

*N*ow, the beige lobby holds no one except for a clerk behind the registration desk at the far end of the room and one bored bellman, who waits patiently at the elevator door with my bag. The registration desk is tiny. There are only two clerks for registration and checkout. Of course, the hotel has been open only a month, and it has been a soft opening, at that; the official opening is a few days off. But still.

At the Taft, we had four check-in clerks and three check-out cashiers and two or three clerks to hand you your key and your mail. In addition to the newsstand and the largest bar in New York, we had a theater ticket counter, a flower shop, a beauty parlor, a six-chair barbershop, a Western Union counter, a Latin American desk (a kind of Spanish-speaking concierge), a public stenographer, a credit manager's office (this was before credit cards, when it took three days' advance notice to cash a check), a coffee shop with a couple of dozen tables and a counter with twenty stools, a jewelry stand, and the porter's room, where luggage was stored. There was a doorman at the main entrance on Seventh Avenue, as well as the one on Fifty-first Street, a dozen bellmen, half a dozen elevator operators, Miss Allen, the assistant manager, and easy chairs, sofas, tables, ashtrays, and floor lamps for about fifty people. No wonder my life has since seemed thin.

I get in the elevator; the bellman asks "What floor?" It's difficult to convey how shocking it is that he doesn't say "please." "Please" was a constant in my childhood, whether it was needed or not, as in "Next stop, fifth floor, please." The double please wasn't unusual, as in "Please face the front of the car, please." Then, "Fifth floor, please. Getting out, please. Let them out, please. Next floor, please." Now it's just "What floor?" My father would have pulled his arms off, would have twisted his head like a cork till it came off his neck, would have given him a *look*.

Behind the old bronze doors, the new elevator is faster than the manual ones I grew up with, faster even than the automatic ones put in after the war. The car fits the shaft with narrower tolerances, and the doors at each floor shut tighter, so that the low moan of air rushing by the car is gone—a lovely, loonlike sound that I didn't miss or even remember until this minute.

I follow the bellman out of the car. Despite the remodeling, the corridors remain narrow. When Peter and I got off on the fifteenth floor and raced home, we often jostled each other into the walls so hard we'd be rubbing our shoulders when we rang the doorbell.

The bellman and I pass a maid and houseman who bow and shrink against the wall to give us room. They are Asian. Until I was twelve, maids were mostly Irish. With the war, the supply of young women from Ireland ceased and those already here applied for better jobs in defense plants. By the end of the war, maids were mostly black. Hotels have always been way stations on the road to the American dream, and hotel kids grow up with daily proof of upward mobility. Dalmatia, a night maid with too little English to work the day shift, put four sons through college, one through medical school. In the hall, the other maids always greeted her respectfully.

When I called the Michelangelo for a reservation, I asked for the manager and explained who I was. I was shocked that he had never heard of Father. He graciously offered to comp me, anyway. (That's short for complimentary, a free room.) After the war, when Father and Mother traveled to Europe, they were comped by grande luxe palace hotels. Their managers knew Father by reputation and were more impressed by the Taft's high occupancy than by the royal names written in spidery purple ink on their own prewar guest registers. When they didn't comp him, he said, they gave him a 50 percent discount—on a suite that cost double what he would have spent for a standard room. Being comped was even more expensive, he said, because of the princely tipping that was then expected.

Handing the bellman a princely tip, I look around a suite decorated in high hotel drama: that is, oversized art objects on bureaus without drawers and on shelves empty of purpose. A divider bookcase, holding an enormous TV, separates the sitting room from the bedroom. The bathroom is also divided in two: one half has a sink, a hair dryer, a tiny TV set, and a bathroom scale. The other half holds a giant soaking tub. One half was probably the original entry to the room when it was just an inexpensive single, the kind a high-school teacher, chaperoning her senior class, would have reserved for herself. The other half must have been the original bathroom.

Our bathrooms were so compact that when the shower was turned on, it sucked the cold shower curtain around your body. A cabinet behind the mirror over the sink stored extra toilet paper—rectangular packets of sheets held together with a paper wrapper—and a neat stack of tiny bars of Ivory soap, each good for a day or two, wrapped in paper printed with the Taft logo. I took the tiny bars to camp, to boarding school, to college. I never bought a bar of soap in my life until I went to Europe in my mid-twenties. Mother probably would have packed cartons of tiny Taft soap bars in my luggage, but I was going to be away too long.

Over the hot and cold water taps, a gooseneck faucet released ice water cold enough to hurt your teeth. Returning home from a visit to relatives uptown, I told Mother, sadly, that they were poor. I had found only two faucets in their bathroom—one for hot and another for cold. No ice water faucet. As fancy as it is, the Michelangelo doesn't offer ice water either, I am pleased to note.

I lie down on the Michelangelo's oversized bed and put my face against the wall. I breathe in deeply but fail to find the particular cool, spicy, satisfying odor of the hard plaster walls of my childhood. I've been pressing my nose into hotel walls for fifty years trying to recapture that smell. It would take me back half a century in a second. Maybe it wasn't the smell of the plaster but the paint. The rooms at the Taft were pale egg-yolk yellow. There was no need to vary the color; guests didn't—or weren't supposed to—wander into other guests' bedrooms. Only our living room was painted a different color: powder blue. The hotel paint shop may have bought the paint just for us.

Sniffing around the bed like an inquisitive dog, I miss the dusty smell of the chenille bedspreads. The blanket doesn't smell like real wool. The sheets smell of the same detergent I recognize from every motel corridor I've ever walked down. Detergent didn't exist when I was young. Our sheets smelled of soap and starch and boiling water. They were changed every day. I'd still like to put my head on a crisp, freshly ironed pillowslip each night and sleep between freshly ironed sheets. Who wouldn't?

When I get up and look out the window south to Fiftieth Street I see that the block across the street has been leveled to the ground. A construction fence surrounds the empty lot. It isn't difficult to guess what happened. A real estate boomlet had persuaded a developer to buy and raze the block. Interest rates rose and caught him overextended. Now he's licking his wounds, waiting for rates to go down again. Developers in New York have short memories that never seem to reach back to the previous recession.

I remember an electric sign on the second floor of a low building across the street that advertised the Gypsy Tea Room. A Woolworth's on the ground floor had a toy counter where Peter and I first bought, later shoplifted, yo-yos, model tanks, tin soldiers, and inexpensive kaleidoscopes. A cigar store on the corner had a gas jet mounted on its counter for customers who wanted to light the cigar they had just purchased. It burned all the time with a steady flame, whether anyone was lighting a cigar or not.

Peter and I admired the flamboyant extravagance of it all and checked the flame, blue on the bottom, orange at the tip, each time we passed.

The Michelangelo's new windows fit better than the old ones did. Though I am on a low floor, the only sound I hear now from the street, faintly, is a crosstown bus, changing gears. The rumble of traffic—a constant throughout my childhood, even ten floors higher than I am now —has disappeared, like the United Cigar Store's eternal flame.

efore we were old enough for school, Peter and I awakened to the sounds of horses' hooves echoing up from the street, through the hotel courtyards. Wagon-loads of food and drink were being delivered to the hotel's sidewalk elevator on Fifty-first Street. Corrugated metal doors flush with the sidewalk would fold outward, and a wooden platform smelling of the dank pantries and halls below would rise to street level, then descend with sides of beef, long, institution-sized loaves of white bread, and produce. In the thirties, Manhattan was crowded with automobiles, trucks, and trolleys, and we were in Manhattan's very heart; yet until the Second World War, junkmen, milkmen, and scissors grinders all made their way through midtown behind slow, tired horses.

Gradually, the other sounds of the city would reach our window—the elevated trains on Sixth Avenue, car horns, workmen shouting to each other, a fire engine's siren, and finally the hum of pedestrian traffic as the city woke. In winter, we lay under warm covers, listening to the radiators spit and hiccup to life. In summer, a decade before air conditioning, I'd spend a minute with my face pressed against the wall, enjoying the chill of the plaster. My bed was separated from Peter's by a night table holding a built-in radio and a hotel telephone. The radio was really a remote speaker operated from the radio room just under the roof. It played only four stations and Muzak. Less expensive than a real radio, it had the additional advantage of not working outside the hotel if a guest pilfered it. The radio room shut down at ten at night so that guests would not be disturbed. The room telephone had no dial; switchboard operators placed our calls. Mother thought they sometimes listened in. I know they must have kept an eye on the switchboard all the time; we never had to wait more than two rings for an operator to answer.

Behind our headboards, a window faced other rooms across the courtyard. If guests forgot to pull down their shades when they undressed, Peter and I peeked at them. Beyond the foot of our beds, a window to the east looked over the roof of the Roxy Theater. When days turned warm, we leaned out over the sill to spy on chorus girls in two-piece bathing suits sunbathing directly below. Sometimes they played catch—a bucolic fantasy on a tar roof to help them break the monotony of six shows a day.

Once I saw Peter stir, I'd race him to the bathroom. Its floor was paved in small octagonal tiles. A bathmat with a green stripe down the middle had "Hotel Taft" woven in white into the stripe. The walls were covered in white porcelain bricks. In front of the toilet, at eye level if you were sitting on the toilet, one brick was printed PLEASE DO NOT THROW ANYTHING IN TOILET WHICH CAN CAUSE OVERFLOW OR DAMAGE. Behind the shower curtain, at eye level if you were standing in the shower, another brick was printed PLEASE PLACE CURTAIN INSIDE TUB WHEN USING SHOWER.

If we did not get up, Bridie would come in and push us out of bed. "Come on, come on. Are youse going to stay in bed all day?" Bridie was a floor maid, released from half of her regular assignment of sixteen rooms so that she could spend half her day in our apartment. We were in our bathrobes by the time we heard squeaky wheels announce the arrival of the room service table in the corridor outside. The waiter knocked softly; Mother was still sleeping. Bridie quietly let him in the entry hall, which was furnished with a two-legged console table that held a vase of dried eucalyptus leaves and a Japanese plate that served as an ashtray. To the waiter's left, a small bedroom held an easy chair and a single bed. At first, a baby nurse slept there, and later, our grandmother. To the waiter's right, the hall led to the living room door, now shut.

Directly in front of him was our bedroom. He maneuvered the room service table into the narrow space between the foot of our beds and the bathroom door. With a flourish, he removed the starched white napkin that lay on top of glasses of ice water, next to glasses of milk, crowding glasses of orange juice nesting in bowls of shaved ice. Buttered toast stayed warm under an aluminum cover with a hole in the center to allow steam to escape. Eggs, hot cereal, or pancakes with sage-scented sausages sat in a heater underneath the table.

Bridie sat with us while we ate. She poured milk on our cereal, stirred it if it was too hot, stopped us from smearing egg yolks on our plates or playing with the brown lace edges around the whites, told us to stop kicking our chair legs. In our pajamas, Peter and I talked on and on, God knows about what, since we had spent the previous day talking together and every day before that. An hour later, when the waiter returned to take the table away, we were dressed in short pants, shirts, and ties. (I didn't own long pants until I was eleven and didn't wear a sports shirt, except in the country, until I went to college.) As the waiter rolled the table out into the hall, Peter slipped a few cubes of sugar into his pocket to feed any horses we might meet on our way to Central Park.

When Mother awoke, between nine and ten, she lit a cigarette and picked up the phone. "Operator, could you please tell me the correct time?" There was only one clock in our suite and the only thing about it that ran were the shepherds and maidens across its front. We must have asked for the time a dozen times a day. Then she'd ask for the weather forecast, the one beginning "United States Weather Bureau forecast for New York City and vicinity." If the operator volunteered that it had been raining or bitter cold when she had come in that morning, Mother would thank her but ask to be connected to the Weather Bureau. After she listened to the forecast, she'd light another cigarette and go into the bathroom. After her bath, she'd put her nightgown back on, open the bedroom door, and return to bed. When we heard the door open, we ran the dozen feet down the hall into the living room and her bedroom, just beyond the living room door.

Unlike the rest of the apartment, which was furnished with indestructible hotel furniture, Mother's bedroom was decorated in antiques or maybe reproductions. She and Father slept in a double bed with a curlicued headboard painted pale green, decorated with nymphs and shepherds, and webbed with a network of fine cracks due to age or a decorator. Bureaus on either side of the bed and a highboy against the opposite wall were part of the same set, probably a wedding gift. The bureaus were beautifully veneered, with faux marble tops. The furniture men periodically refinished them because of the cigarettes that rolled off Mother's cloisonné ashtray to smolder on the wood. Drawn window shades shut off her view of the Empire State Building a mile away.

In her silk nightgown, her head propped against the headboard, a phone in one hand, a cigarette in the other, she'd smile and wave to us when we entered. Strong-featured rather than pretty, she had a large nose, long teeth, and wiry hair that turned gray late and stayed salt-and-pepper until she died. I inherited her long storky legs. Lying on her back in bed, she'd crook one leg over the other, at right angles, like a man sitting. Under the bed-clothes, they formed a tent. We leaned over to kiss her cheek, which smelled of sleep and tobacco, and sat on the bed. If Grandma Esther—her mother—was staying with us, she joined us, too, in an easy chair near the window. She'd be already dressed for the day, corseted, in a shape-less dark dress.

We'd listen to Mother on the phone with her sister-in-law, Mickey. Best friends from camp days, they had con-spired to marry Mick to Mother's brother, Corny. Mick and Corny had a daughter my age, whom I saw often, and a son a few years older, handsome and taciturn. Mother called Mickey every morning. Because she said the number aloud to the operator every day for so many years, it is the only phone number from my childhood, beside my own, that I still remember. Sometimes she'd affect the broad

British *a* the two girls had learned taking diction lessons together a few years before. Mick kept the *a;* Mother used hers only on the phone with Mick. We sat quietly, listening to Mother's half of the conversation until it was more than she could stand. "My God! Haven't you people anything to do? Get out!" Although she has hit the nail on the head—none of us had anything to do at all—Grandmother would march out in a huff and we'd follow, pestering her for stories about the old days in the shtetl where she was born. Her father had run a crossroads country store and bootlegged on the side. She told of a step-brother, chased by Jew-hating peasants, who escaped onto the roof of their store, fell off, and died. Her favorite sister fell in love with a Cossack. After his troop came to destroy their stock of vodka, smashing the barrels and flooding the floor with the illegal alcohol, the lover returned secretly and helped the family mop the vodka up and put it back into new barrels. When she told us this, Peter and I made faces, disgusted at the unsanitary state of the vodka her father's customers were offered. Esther looked at us as if we were idiots. "Boys, boys. What did they know? They were peasants." All this she told us in a Yiddish accent, strong and sweet as tea, until it was time for the maid to take us up to the roof to play or to the park.

Mother went out rarely. She had little reason to. The valet picked up our laundry and dry cleaning. The newsstand sent up cigarettes or magazines. If she needed cash for tips—the only money she needed, since she signed for everything else—the cashier sent it upstairs and she signed for that, too. She made fun of women who dressed up just to go shopping for clothes. If she needed something, she'd call a saleswoman she knew at Saks Fifth Avenue. She'd describe what she thought she might like; the saleswoman would describe some dresses back to her and send over half a dozen on approval. For years, I thought all adults bought their clothes on approval. Choosing one, or more often, none, she'd tell Bridie to return the rest to the package room, where Robbins the Package Boy would repack them, ready for the store to pick up.

Bridie made the beds, picked up dirty ashtrays, brought Mother a glass of water, kept her company. She wielded great power in the hotel because of the many hours she and Mother spent together. What she knew about our family was valuable currency in the halls and locker rooms, while the gossip she heard, which she might choose to pass on to Mother, could, others worried, help or hurt them. Her style was energetic and angular, her body as sharp-edged as her tongue. She showed Peter and me much of what we knew of the world outside the Taft, once taking us on the train to Sing Sing to visit her husband, a prison guard. Another time, she took us for the weekend to the tiny apartment she and her husband rented in Brooklyn. We marveled at her ingenuity when we saw milk and butter on the ledge outside her window, eliminating the need for an icebox. She worked late, often giving us our evening bath before leaving the hotel for the day. It never occurred to us how late it must have been when she got home, how little she and her husband saw each other.

A little before noon, Mother put on rouge and lipstick and combed her wiry hair again. She put on a fresh night-gown and a quilted robe. Friends called from the lobby or rang our doorbell: Mick, Mick's sister, Lee, aunts or cousins in for the day from Jersey. Mother never knew who was coming, nor did any of her friends or family need to call. Every day was open house. At noon, a room service table was wheeled into the living room, which was striped with bright light from windows on three sides. The living room held a hard hotel sofa, a couple of easy chairs, and side chairs covered in leatherette, the kind you find in conference rooms.

The table was a tight squeeze, especially set for six, as it was each day. It held a huge platter of cold roast beef, ham, sliced chicken, and turkey breast, enough of each so that six guests could all have just chicken, if they wanted, or could all have roast beef. Sliced tomatoes and a bowl of lettuce, washed and separated into leaves, sat next to platters lined with sliced rye and white bread. If, rarely, more than six people showed up, Bridie went into the tiny kitchenette next to the living room, converted from the original bathroom there, and took more china and silver from a white enamel cupboard. After everyone had finished, Bridie would help herself to the platters and take her sandwich out to the locker room. Mother's favorite story was about a man, invited by a friend, overcome by the magnificence of the spread. "And you have this every day? You must divorce Alfred and marry me!" The woman who had brought him laughed. "You idiot, the lunch doesn't come with her, it comes with him!"

This daily lunch enabled Mother never to lack company. Friends who worked downtown might drop in for a quick bite, but most of her visitors had little to do and were glad to spend the afternoon. The room service table was removed and Bridie would set up a bridge table for a card game. They'd play canasta or gin rummy, for points, not money, just something to fill the hours until evening. They played cards until someone looked at a watch and said, "My God! Bernie will kill me."

"Not so fast," Mother would say, not looking up from her cards. "Make him take you out. Let's just finish this game. I'm on a winning streak."

Three or four times a year, a middle-aged blonde woman, powerfully built, would come to the suite with a portable table and give Mother a massage. "No cards this afternoon," she'd tell her friends at lunch. "I'm having a massage."

If she couldn't persuade anyone to stay after lunch, she'd call Dolly, who, with her husband, Al, owned the hotel newsstand. Peter and I called them Aunt Dolly and Uncle Al—they were courtesy relatives only, though we did not know that at first and continued to call them that until we were grown. When, years later, I saw *Guys and Dolls,* I realized Uncle Al was a dead ringer for practically everyone in the show except the Salvation Army heroine and the chorus girls at the Hot Box. He was well under six feet tall and weighed over 250 pounds. He wore checked sports jackets and shirts a size or two larger than necessary. Dolly seemed too elegant to sell newspapers and candy from behind a counter. She had a beauty spot like a Hungarian movie star and was proud of a special combination of perfumes she had devised for herself: Joy behind her ears, Arpege at her throat, Chanel somewhere else. It was unique and very complicated. As soon as we got off the elevator on the fifteenth floor, Peter and I could tell if Dolly was visiting, a hundred yards down the hall. If Mother didn't feel like playing cards, Dolly would keep her company in the bedroom. She had a ready smile and nodded agreeably as Mother talked.

Although concessions like the newsstand paid rent, their owners often acted as if Father were an important client, not the other way around. Perhaps the rents were low. Certainly, few hotels were as busy as ours, providing the lobby traffic that the newsstand, the jewelry counter, and the flower shop needed to stay in business.

When Mother couldn't persuade friends to stay after lunch and she didn't feel like seeing Dolly, she'd make Peter play cards with her. He was a good card player, even when he was eight or nine. He'd sit at the table with his shoes off, rubbing one foot against his other leg, concentrating on his hand. When he was winning she'd send him out of the room for a glass of water and cheat. Years later, she told him. "I worried that you'd become a gambler like my father. Remember how you liked to bet on the horses?" Peter used to place dime bets on the horses at Aqueduct with Uncle Al. When Peter didn't want to play cards, Mother would pull down the silk coverlet on her bed and deal herself hands of solitaire on the blanket until it was time for Father to come upstairs.

When I was sick—I was kept in bed with bronchitis and asthma a lot—Mother would wake up early, hover over my bed, and put her warm palm on my forehead. She took my temperature often and told Chef to make me orange Jell-O with real orange juice. I'd listen to the radio: *Life Can Be Beautiful, The Romance of Helen Trent,* the same soap operas Esther listened to in the next room. I'd have lunch in bed.

With Peter at school, there was nothing for me to do. The comic books Aunt Dolly sent up from the newsstand would be finished in an hour. When I heard the front door in the hall open and Peter's voice call out, I would sit up, eager to talk with him, but he wasn't allowed in. He'd peek in at me, a worried look on his face, and ask me how I was, but even from her bedroom Mother could tell he was there. "Peter. You stay out of there! That's all I need, both of you sick!" Looking apologetic, he'd softly close the door. The day seemed endless, and I'd get some faint sense of the emptiness of Mother's days.

At first, before we were old enough for school, even before we were allowed to leave the apartment by ourselves, Peter and I went to the roof with a nursemaid. Peter hated to take his hat off in the elevator because his curly, dazzlingly platinum blond hair made women exclaim, "What I wouldn't give for hair like that!" We called him Harpo. (Once he asked Father, "Do carrots make curls?" and Father answered, "No, ice cream does.") Peter's face, even as an infant, was questioning and alert. Mother called him "Monkey Face." It was accepted in our family that I would be well over six feet tall and that he wouldn't. He hated being short, he hated his curly hair, and I can't imagine he liked being called Monkey Face.

Getting off on the twenty-first floor, we walked past the paint shop, smelling of turpentine, the furniture refinishing shop, pungent with shellac, and the valet, a room full of steam and dry-cleaning fluid in place of air. A hotel has thousands of smells, and our noses, new as puppies', knew them all. An iron door with a rusted handle opened onto the roof. Exiting it was like walking onto the upper deck of a steamship. The roof was interrupted by small mysteries: ventilation ducts, iron ladders four or five steps high, leading from level to level for no apparent reason, tiny terraces checkerboarded around housings for mechanical systems. An electric sign spelling "Hotel Taft" reached fifty feet above the roof. It was angled so that it faced south down Seventh Avenue and west toward the Hudson. We had a slide, a sandbox, a fire engine with pedals. We played carefully, watched by nurses who warned us not to step on the soft tar lines that crisscrossed everywhere, or pick at the tar, or get our hands dirty climbing the rusty ladders.

In place of a reality too remote for me to distinguish its details, I remember a photograph of a plain woman in a starched white dress on the roof, watching over us. We are spotless. During the Depression, nurses were willing to work for only a few dollars, but we had little money our- selves. When money was tight, nannies were replaced by hotel maids, who watched over us at odd hours or in the evening. Then, as our parents thought they saw money on the horizon, the maids were replaced by new nannies, who were in turn replaced by maids again when the money disappeared. Whenever blue-uniformed hotel maids replaced the nannies in starched white, we took advantage of the lapse in discipline to get as dirty as we could.

When we got old enough to roam the hotel by our- selves, we played within a cat's cradle of rules that only hotel kids know. The first rule was not to disturb the guests, faceless, irritable, always dozing, like cats. "You'll wake the guests." Day or night, doorknobs were hung with "Do Not Disturb" signs. We'd hush as we came upon one, stay silent exactly the width of the door, then begin laughing and chattering as soon as we passed the door frame.

The second rule was "Don't go outside." Seventh Av- enue was a twenty-four-hour-a-day parade of trucks, cars, trolleys, pickpockets, drunks, and child molesters. Like all kids, we were supposed to find something to do, but un- like others, we were permanently grounded. That rule was backed up by doormen, bellmen, house dicks, and porters. Forbidden to leave the building, we ran down

Peter and I on the hotel roof around 1934 and in a studio portrait in 1936. We are seventeen months apart in age, and it was intensely annoying to him that from my birthday at the end of May until his in late October, I was "two" years older.

Postcards such as these were available at the front desk, in the guest rooms, and at the desks in the writing area on the mezzanine.

basement corridors smelling damply of discarded greens, raced each other up and down the inside fire stairs, and invented games on the roof that made Seventh Avenue, with its putative perverts and pickpockets, childproof by comparison. We climbed parapets and ladders and attempted to crawl down the steam vents. As we gained confidence, we climbed the maintenance ladder alongside the lighted Taft sign. The older we grew, the higher we climbed, though neither of us ever had the nerve to climb to the top. Not that it made much difference; the bottom rung was twenty-one stories above the street.

We roamed the lobby. Although transient guests were drops of water in a changing stream, there were a number of permanents we saw frequently. During the Depression, it was unimaginably hard to fill the rooms. Desperate, Father charged only thirty dollars a month for the very smallest ones. Perhaps because of the size of the rooms, the permanent guests were small, too. I remember a lady four and a half feet tall who walked through the lobby three times a day with a Chihuahua; a larger dog wouldn't have fit in a thirty-dollar-a-month room. The Chihuahua ignored us when we talked to its mistress and snapped at us when we tried to pet it. The woman, in her mid-thirties, maybe even forty, wore little girls' clothes. Perhaps she couldn't find adult clothes her size, but she wore a little girl's hat, too, with a big black grosgrain bow.

Even smaller was an actor who called the Taft home between engagements in a road company tour of *Snow White and the Seven Dwarfs*. When we ran up to him, he'd tell us about the towns he had played. "Cincinnati, it's on the river. Nice town. Good audiences." One afternoon, we called Mother from a house phone in the lobby and asked if we could bring a friend upstairs. Years later, she told us how surprised she'd been, opening the door to see a man not much taller than we, wearing a fedora. He came in, sat on the sofa, his legs dangling, eating ice cream and chain-smoking. Mother enjoyed his show biz talk and invited him back, but he never came upstairs again. When we grew taller than he, he pretended not to see us, and we learned to stop saying hello.

Our third rule was not to pester employees. But many of them were glad to interrupt the mindless monotony of hotel work. On slow days, the black bellmen waited forever at the bell captain's desk, the Greek and German room service waiters sat for hours on broken chairs in an airless hall outside the hot kitchen, the porters lounged on trunks in the storage room, lying about their property back home in Ireland. We snatched the waiters' service napkins and ran. We grabbed Tony the Porter's hat and badge. As he was gaining on us, we threw them down the incinerator chute. He protected us as long as he could but was finally forced to explain what had happened to hat and badge. "Djou little boys was so fast. I don' know how djou could run so fast," he laughed years later, tickled to tell us about the hat and badge, even when we were nearly grown.

If the elevator operator was a friend, like Bob, a light-skinned, redheaded black man with a string of freckles across his face, we rode the car up until the last guest got off. We'd whine and pull at Bob's rough wool trouser leg. "No, no, no. Your father, he'd kill me. You know you ain't s'pose to play in the elevator." He'd sigh. "You know, he finds out, he's gonna kill me, so be careful, now."

There was a brass handle to push forward or pull back along the circumference of a round disk mounted on the car wall, like a ship's engine-room telegraph. Depending on how far the handle was moved, forward or back, the car rose or fell, slower or faster. When released, it swung naturally to twelve o'clock on the disk, and the elevator coasted to a stop. It took time to learn to align the floor of the elevator with the sill of the floor outside. New men, who were nauseated by the constant up and down their entire first week anyway, would jiggle the brass handle, jarring passengers in a particularly annoying way as they raised and lowered the elevator an inch at a time before finally getting it right. Bob leaned against the elevator wall and watched with amusement as Peter and I accelerated quickly, the pitch of the wind past the door rising as the car went faster. We could release the brass handle, often as far as a floor away from our destination, and coast, without further adjustment, into perfect alignment with the sill.

Peter and I visited Charlie the Steward in his basement pantry. He guarded shelves of institution-sized canned goods and a walk-in meat refrigerator where we could shiver among sides of aging beef and limp chickens. Charlie had come from Greece as a young man and had worked for Father longer than anyone else. He saved us the little plastic white horses on ribbons that used to hang from White Horse Scotch bottles, and the little black and white Scotties from bottles of Black and White Scotch—hotel kid toys. If any child had more of those than we did, his father owned a liquor store.

After asking us if we had been good, Charlie took us across the hall to Paul the Pastry Chef, a tall, smiling Dane whose sweet-smelling kitchen led to a walk-in refrigerator as large as our bedroom—larger—lined with wire racks of breakfast pastries, eclairs, napoleons, yellow and chocolate cakes, and pies. The racks, rising almost to the ceiling, held half a dozen shelves, each holding in turn perhaps thirty chocolate eclairs, topped by three more shelves of mocha eclairs, next to twenty or thirty fruit pies. Paul, who was taller than Father, had to stand on a step stool to bring down pastries from the top rack. He fed us napoleons and cinnamon buns; Charlie liked to feed us eclairs himself, pushing them into our mouths with a thumb so garlicky that all eclairs since seem to lack a certain élan. We ate so much pastry that fifty years later, neither Peter nor I eat dessert much.

Unlike employees everywhere else in the hotel, the kitchen workers looked at Peter and me from under angry brows. There are a hundred ways to get hurt in a kitchen; they were probably scared we would get burned, scalded, bruised, or cut and they'd be blamed. At the far end of the kitchen, behind flaming ovens and clouds of steam, Chef sat at his desk in black checked pants and a towering toque. When he saw us, he would get up, greet us cordially, and pat our heads while walking us toward the door. In a minute we'd find ourselves back in the corridor, feeling aggrieved. If we had gotten hurt in the kitchen, we wouldn't have said anything. Once when I was older, on one of the few evenings Mother assumed we were old enough to be left alone, Peter and I were playing with knives. I cut myself badly. The Grill Room captain approached Mother where she and Father were dining with friends. He thought she should know that I had called the switchboard and asked the operator to find the hotel doctor. I had told the operator, the captain said to Mother, that it was a matter of life and death, but not to bother my parents.

Like all royalty, we grew up distrusting flattery or even compliments. I learned later that the people with whom I was most comfortable, with whom I felt most secure—Charlie the Steward, Smitty the Waiter, Tony the Porter—had all worked for Father before the Taft. They had been waiting for us when Mother and Father brought me home from the hospital, had known me, as they sometimes said, since before I was born.

As we grew older, we invited school friends back to the hotel to play. Hotel kids don't play the games other kids do. We didn't play baseball or touch football. In childhood snapshots, Peter holds his hand ineffectually above his eyes, squinting into the sun. His shirttail hangs out. I am taller and have a potbelly. Neither of us is anyone that anyone on a playground would pick for his team until everyone else had been chosen. (I was twenty-six years old, playing catch with friends at the beach, when my girlfriend looked carefully at the way the little red rubber ball bounced out of my hands whenever I tried to catch it. She stopped the game and taught me how to pull my arms in toward my chest so that the ball wouldn't keep bouncing out of my outstretched hands like that.) But we were unbeatable at hotel games—Silent Corridor Running, which our friends lost, not by running slower down the maze of jogs and bypasses that we knew so well, but by yelling when they crashed into an unexpected wall after a sharp turn. And they risked throwing up if they tried to compete with us in Elevator Free-Fall. Sometimes they begged us to stop even before it was their turn to take the brass handle.

But we all spent most of our days in the apartment, which, from the eucalyptus leaves on the table in the front hall to the farthest end of the living room, was less than fifty steps. Father was very modest and hated having anyone in his bedroom if he wanted to use the bathroom. Too embarrassed to ask us to leave, he'd look pleadingly at Mother until she caught on and asked us to go. Usually, we automatically closed doors behind us. Even so, a continual unfolding of coughs, farts, radio programs, and flushing toilets announced us to each other. Our doorbell rang a dozen times a day, bringing menus, meals, ice, cigarettes. Housemen, carpet cleaners, electricians, furniture polishers, bellmen, and valets fixed, cleaned, or picked things up. Only Bridie could disappear when she needed to, slipping out to the maid's locker room for a smoke.

When Mother had company, Peter and I stayed in our room and played pick-up sticks or battled tin soldiers on the carpet until our knees grew rashes. He was more literal than I, and I had to be careful about setting up the scenario of our games. If the battered figures we arrayed on the carpet were soldiers from some unspecified war this week, it would be two more weeks before I could persuade Peter that they were now cowboys and Indians. "He's got no pretend," I once complained.

Peter and I missed our privacy, especially when we fought. We argued quietly. When one of us punched the other, we tried to punch quietly, neither of us making a sound that someone in the next room might hear. We couldn't storm out of the room; all the other rooms were occupied, too, by Mother or Grandmother or Bridie. I learned to tune out. When I wanted to be somewhere else, I listened to the radio, or read, or lay on my bed staring at the ceiling, humming. When things are unpleasant, I'm still able to slip effortlessly away, like Leslie Howard in *The Scarlet Pimpernel*.

Friends and relatives, oblivious to the possibility that we might be busy, sick, or fighting, felt free to visit unannounced. If they called at all, it would be from a house phone in the lobby. As often as not, they'd just show up at our door. Mother once asked the maid to tell some out-of-town relatives waiting at the front door that she wasn't in—but I walked past them as Bridie delivered the message. They asked about school, and Peter. Just then, Mother walked by in her nightgown. Their mouths dropped. Mother's opened too, to scream—at them or at me—"Close the goddamned door!" I closed the door behind me, locking myself out in the hall with them. They smiled awkwardly and retreated, back to the elevators, leaving me alone in the corridor.

Once, when she decided that we had too much privacy—I must have been seven or eight—Mother began walking around the apartment nearly naked. She had heard somewhere that unsatisfied curiosity about the naked human body was not healthful for young boys and girls. She may have misunderstood some half-digested scrap of Freudian insight at a cocktail party. She was not a good listener, although she looked like one: her face alight, her head cocked in alert appreciation, her mind wandering. Bright and talkative, she could carry on a lively discourse, full of strongly held opinions, leavened with almost no actual information. Isolated in the apartment, not a reader, before television, she picked up ideas God knows where with no way to check them out. To her, evolution and levitation were equally likely—or implausible.

Since we had no sisters to show us breasts, she decided it was up to her. Leaving the doors open when she took a bath, she'd call us in to hand her a hairbrush or the soap. After a very short while, when she called us in, we pretended not to hear. She took to walking around the apartment in a sheer nightgown. (First she made sure the shades were drawn—she didn't feel like satisfying the curiosity of hotel guests, too.) Finally, Grandma Esther came up from Florida to spend the summer. The thought of explaining to her own mother what she was doing daunted even Mother, and she went back to bathing with her door shut.

When Mother and Father fought, Peter and I poised like sprinters, ready to dash for our room at the first "Goddamn it!" Esther turned her radio up as loud as it would go. If Mother sensed an awkward stillness after a particularly noisy argument, she'd say, "Your father doesn't like to be yessed. He could have had any number of silly girls who would have said, 'Of course, Alfred, whatever you say, Alfred,' couldn't you, dear?" Although their fighting upset the rest of us, it didn't bother them. Whether they ended their day laughing or shouting or whispering, they always made sure to lock their bedroom door when they went to bed, and Esther, Peter, and I ignored any sounds that came from their room after that.

three

*W*ithin the hotel, we were rich. Jumbo shrimp, bottles of Scotch, and freshly ironed sheets were ours without limit. Out on the street, though, money was tight. If our parents wanted to go out for dinner, they went to the basement Grill Room. There were very few places where we would eat better food or receive better treatment than right downstairs in our own restaurant, they often said, our very own Taft Grill. Like many restaurants designed in the twenties, it was decorated in what was called the "Spanish effect" (accurate only if houses in Spain boasted revolving colored gels in the ceiling and Moorish columns twined with plaster vines). Grillrooms were a popular way then to profit from what otherwise would have been just a basement.

There were three ways to go to the Grill, each with its own special satisfaction. On hot summer days, I most enjoyed entering from Seventh Avenue. When the pavement shimmered in clear sunlight, the stairway that led down to the Grill was a haven of cool darkness. My eyes adjusted slowly to the dim light, so that the room always appeared magically.

Mother's favorite way was by elevator from the fifteenth floor directly to the basement. But only half the cars went that far, so a third way down involved taking the elevator to the lobby, then walking across the lobby to the marble stairs next to the barbershop. No more than two dozen steps—but before we got there, the bellmen, porters, and elevator operators were buzzing. We were pointed out to new men.

"That's the boss's family."

"I thought Mr. Greene was the boss."

"Nah, nah. That white man there's the big boss!"

"That's his wife? That long drink of water? Those his kids?"

"Yeah."

"They get to eat whatever they want?"

"Yeah. Steaks, ice cream, whatever."

I was immensely proud of Father's formal demeanor and Mother's imposing height. I told friends she was six feet tall. She insisted she was five foot nine, but I think she was taller than that, perhaps halfway between her estimate and mine. When she went to the Grill, she put on a black dress and wore a big picture hat. As we descended the stairs, we heard music rising to greet us, like a parade approaching. When the maitre d', stationed at the podium next to the cloakroom, saw us, he went wild with delight, standing on tiptoe to greet us. "Your reservation is ready," he sang out if there were customers waiting on line, whether we had reserved or not. A captain led us to our table and seated us, gathering Mother's cloth coat off her shoulders as if it were chinchilla, delicately dropping our napkins in our laps as if our groins were glass. A young woman in an abbreviated skirt and net stockings, walking from table to table with a muffin warmer hanging from her neck, instantly appeared. She smiled radiantly at Peter and me and, delving deep with silver tongs, deposited small, warm, sticky honey buns on our butter plates.

Smitty the Waiter came over. He'd take my napkin and turn it into a white linen rabbit. Twisting its tail, he made it jump into my lap. He could also turn the napkin into a brassiere which he modeled for us on his shirtfront. As we grew older, he stopped doing the bra trick; then, when we were considerably older and bringing dates to the Grill, he started it again. He had left Greece at the age of fourteen, he told us, after his father had hit him.

Heavily carpeted, the room hummed with conversation, the clink of glasses and silverware, and music. Thickly padded swinging doors, designed to soundproof against the shouts of waiters trying to outshout other waiters, led to and from the kitchen. The waiters jostled and joked as they tried to get their orders in ahead of the others'. When they picked up their orders, they'd snatch the fourth slice of lamb off the leg-of-lamb dinner, if they could—stuffing it into their mouths and swallowing it nearly whole as they carefully wiped the margins of the plate with a napkin and rearranged the broccoli with their fingers—before walking out, sedate but speedy, through the padded swinging doors.

In front of the bandstand at the other end of the room, a young man and woman sat on straightback chairs: band singers waiting their turn at the microphone, their hands clasped in their laps, tapping their toes and smiling at the dancers on the floor. The bandleader might have been George Hall, a Paul Whiteman look-alike who brushed his thinning hair straight back the same way, with singer Dolly Dawn and her Dawn Patrol or Enoch Light and his Light Brigade or Ben Bernie, or Frankie Masters or Vincent Lopez. (For a while, mercifully short, Mr. Light gave Peter violin lessons.)

Tables were set well apart so that people could easily get up, dance, and go back to their dinners. Tables for two lined the walls, where single guests could eat by themselves, watching everyone else have a good time. Sconces high on the Moorish columns softly lit the tables.

When we celebrated a birthday, the hotel's press agent came to our table with his Speed Graflex. The bandleader came over, too, to have his picture taken with us. Bandleaders played at all my birthday parties and always asked me my favorite song. When, on my sixth birthday, George Hall apologized for not having the arrangement for "San Francisco" and I felt my eyes sting with tears, I dimly realized that I was spoiled.

Birthday dinners were either lamb chops (with paper pants, which could be taken upstairs afterward) or roast beef (with a big bone, which could not). Though each of us ordered according to individual preference, we shared the same traditional birthday dessert: an ice-cream cake with layers of chocolate, vanilla, and strawberry ice cream set between twin layers of thin yellow cake. It arrived with sugar roses, candles, and the name of the birthday boy on top. Along with it came a trio of silver-plated gravy boats filled with chocolate sauce, strawberry sauce—nearly solid with strawberries—and hot fudge sauce. (Actually, we ate the same ice-cream cake as many as four nights a week, though without the candles, the roses, or the three sauces. More than one sauce would have been considered extravagant on a school night.)

One year, an intensely unhappy waiter, delivering shrimp cocktails, whispered in Mother's ear that the birth-

My fourth birthday party, in the Taft Room on the mezzanine next to Father's office, 1935. I am in the center; Peter is on the far-left. I vaguely remember getting tired and cross and punching one of the other boys. After that, we had smaller birthday parties in the Grill.

My twelfth birthday party, in the Taft Grill, 1943. I am standing with bandleader Ben Bernie. Then, counterclockwise, are Mother, Father, "Aunt" Dolly, Grandma Esther, Peter, and two unidentified friends. Note the ubiquitous ice-cream cake.

day cake had disappeared. Concerned looks on the grown-ups' side of the table. Quivering lips on ours. I can guess what hell there was to pay in the kitchen that night. Paul the Pastry Chef, or a sous-chef if Paul had gone home, would have dropped everything else to make a new cake. Anyone who has spent time in a restaurant kitchen knows that harsh words were exchanged. We ate slower and slower to give the kitchen a break. I swung my feet under my chair; I listened to the band and the insistent clink of ice cubes against the back of my teeth as I drank glass after glass of water. Then the cake came, slapped together, candles askew, one layer shifted past the other two, but a birthday cake all the same.

The Tap Room served more casual food than the Grill. It was the hotel's bar. Chairs were upholstered in red leather, and red leather banquettes lined the walls. It was noisier than the Grill—though there was no orchestra, there was lots more drinking, and the higher noise level easily penetrated the heavy glass doors that led into the lobby. The Tap Room was popular with midtown workers dropping in after work. From five in the afternoon until seven, waiters carried big plates of free cubes of cheese, tiny hot dogs, and meatballs to the tables, courtesy of my smart father. I asked, "Won't people fill up on the meatballs and not order dinner?" He said, yes, but no one would stand up, put on his coat, and say, "Let's go. I'm starved."

Big drinks were Father's religion. In the Grill, drinks were an ounce and a quarter; at tables in the Tap Room, they were an ounce and a half; and at the horseshoe-shaped bar itself, where people went to *drink,* they were an ounce and three-quarters. At our table, Father would lean over confidentially and tell me, even when I was only ten, "Customers can tell a stingy drink."

Until after the Second World War, guest rooms weren't air-conditioned; little in Manhattan was. Father kept the Tap Room freezing to lure sweaty pedestrians off Fifty-first Street. On hot nights in summer, we ate there. Sometimes, Father called for an old car he kept in a nearby garage. After dinner, we'd drive up the West Side Highway into Westchester and country-cool night air. Peter and I would fall asleep in the back seat on the way home.

Behind the Tap Room, the Village Room was decorated with real balconies in front of fake windows lit from behind, jutting from walls plastered and patched to look like a Spanish or Italian village—anyway, a village. Across the room, festive lights were strung from wall to wall. A sign on a wall said, "Casa del Gallo," with a rooster painted below it. Candles guttered on red-checked table-cloths. Charley Drew, a good-looking tenor with an ap-

My parents' ninth wedding anniversary, in the Village Room, 1936. Father is at the far end of the table; Mother is at his right (looking to her right). Among other relatives, friends, and employees, I recognize Grandfather Morris, midway down the right-hand side of the picture, wearing pince-nez.

pealing Irish face (Mother, who had met his mother, said he was Czechoslovakian), sang "Songs Teacher Never Taught You," mostly about breasts and bathrooms. For nearly thirty years, his hair an increasingly unlikely color, he sang parodies of popular songs of the day, laden with

DINNER
ALFRED LEW...
EL TAFT - JAN... 19...

heavy-handed double- and even single-entendres. Customers found his songs uproarious. Some I still remember, the lyrics successfully fighting eviction from my brain for half a century. "She had the biggest Kanakas in Hawaii." "I'd like to nibble on your cupcakes." When, in the second verse, he sang "nnnible," women would laugh and laugh. When anyone got up to go to the bathroom, he'd interrupt himself to sing, "We know where you're going." Everyone would laugh. Once he sang it when my mother left the room. When she came back, she was furious. "What's wrong?" I asked. "He always does that." "Not to the manager's wife!" she said.

Mother enjoyed the fuss the waiters and captains made over us, and Peter and I looked forward to the honey buns in the Grill, the tiny meatballs in the Tap Room, and Charley's songs in the Village. But, except on hot summer nights and birthdays, we didn't often eat downstairs; I suppose at the end of the day Mother and Father seldom felt like dressing up to dine among strangers.

My earliest recollection is of Peter eating in his high chair while I sat at a room service table in our bedroom. Probably a sous-chef had puréed meat or vegetables for him. Later, a nurse or Bridie sat with us while we ate an early supper in our bedroom. It arrived on a table pushed by Harry the Waiter, who'd play with us for a few minutes before he lifted the snowy napkins off our sandwiches. Mother would drop in, then go back to finish dressing or join her company in the living room.

They sometimes entertained Mother's relatives, less often Father's. Mother may have felt his family looked down on her family—Russian, not German, Jews. Father's Aunt Lulu came often, though. A difficult woman, she hated rabbis and lawyers. She didn't like doctors, either: though wealthy, when she was ill she took off her jewelry and walked to a nearby free clinic. Mother was very fond of her.

I remember the sound of glasses touching, talk, and laughter a dozen yards away. As everyone left to go down to the Grill, a bubble of voices and laughter would move from the living room through the hall and out the door. Still laughing, someone would slam the door, and we'd hear voices for a minute more, growing fainter, in the corridor on the way to the elevators.

I can't recall a time when I didn't order my own dinner, although Mother or a maid had to recite the menu to me before I learned to read. When we were old enough—ten or eleven—to sit at dinner with our parents as a matter of course, we joined them for cocktails and hors d'oeuvres.

At six, when the doorbell rang, Peter and I raced each other to let the waiter in. When Peter was very young, and I got to the door first, he would fling himself on the floor of the foyer and burst into tears. The understanding waiter would back out, shutting the door behind him, and ring the bell again so that Peter could win, too. It might have been Harry, whose love for us shone out of his big Greek face, or Paul, a slim, melancholy man with a melodic Austrian accent who called out "Vay-tor-r-r" as he entered, a two-note birdcall starting high and ending low, or George, with a deeply pitted face, who never smiled. Mother was afraid of him and called him the Nazi behind his back. Whoever the waiter, he knew what to do; new waiters weren't sent to our apartment. He'd turn the table tightly in the hall and wheel it into the living room, setting it up under a window that looked out on the courtyard.

The table held oval glass raviers of celery and olives, a small round glass bowl (called a nappy) of shrimp resting in a bowl of ice, and slices of pâté or a bowl of chopped chicken livers. If Aunt Mick and Uncle Cor were there, there'd be a bowl of herring in sour cream, too. The waiter rearranged the dishes—an inch to the left, two inches to the right, just enough to show he *cared*.

"Peter, don't inhale the shrimp. Stephen, you're getting cocktail sauce all over your shirt." While they drank whisky or martinis, I sipped ginger ale, sometimes out of a shot glass which I refilled every few minutes. We passed the menu from hand to hand. A fresh menu was printed for lunch and again for dinner every day, folded in the middle to make two full pages. The à la carte section on the left side never varied, listing isolated bits and pieces like Kadota figs, rashers of bacon, and carrots vichy. I couldn't imagine who would order from it. (I still can't.) The table d'hôte listing on the right offered six or seven dishes at lunch; nine or ten at dinner. Many have passed out of fashion—vegetable dinner topped with poached egg, spaghetti Caruso, broiled mackerel.

Traditional European chefs, like ours, chose dishes to keep a traditional French *batterie de cuisine* occupied: something for the fry cook, the roast man, the *saucier,* the *garde manger* in charge of the cold plates. During the Depression, New York restaurants had many talented cooks. One of our chefs had previously cooked for Queen Margherita of Italy. Another was brother to the chef at the Lafayette Hotel, then quite famous. Until I went to summer camp, I did not know that other children didn't eat chicken livers and giblets in Madeira, or steak and kidney pie. Of course, they ate things I had never seen: peanut butter sandwiches, tuna casseroles, macaroni and cheese.

Each of us ordered from a limited number of favorites. Some foods didn't travel well. Crisply broiled chicken turned soggy in the freight elevator; peas turned to pellets. On the other hand, roast beef and creamed spinach seemed to mellow on the way upstairs. Steaks and hamburgers were easiest to choose when nothing else appealed to us. For the manager's family, there wasn't much difference between them. The steak, called sirloin on the menu, was really a shell steak, sometimes called a New York strip or hotel cut. When we ordered a hamburger, that steak was chopped and put on a bun. Paying guests who ordered a burger got ground round.

Long dialogues about what to order filled the cocktail hour. "You had a sandwich last night," Mother would say. "Have a hot meal tonight." Or, "You forgot to order a green salad." She might call Room Service two or three times before we arrived at a final order. "Change the creamed spinach to a big bowl of sliced tomatoes. Make that club sandwich on rye toast. Are the string beans canned? Yes? Cancel them." If Grandma Esther was staying with us, we allowed considerably more time for our predinner dialogue. She was horrified by the prices. That Father didn't pay—he or Mother signed the checks, and so did we when we were old enough—did nothing to lessen her anguish. Each evening she insisted she wasn't hungry. Each evening we had to guess what she wanted. We must have sounded like a team of grotesquely solicitous maitre d's waiting on a very rich, very difficult customer.

"Perhaps some broiled chicken . . . very good . . . with just a little green salad?" She makes a face. "How about a mushroom omelet?" Peter, age eight, pipes up. "That's very light." Another face. We knew she was hungry. She could be stubborn. Tight-lipped, she shook her head, her marcelled gray hair not moving at all, insisting she wanted nothing, before finally giving in.

About once a week, when Mother felt we should settle down to a more disciplined diet, she made us order broiled chicken or filet of sole, overcooked, simultaneously tasteless and fishy. We might have to start or finish with fruit, usually canned fruit cocktail: diced canned peaches and pears, a few canned white grapes, a really nasty canned fig, and a maraschino cherry on top dripping red dye over the rest.

Mother had strong feelings about what was healthy and what was not. Hot sweet rolls were the unhealthiest food people could eat. As a teenager she had once eaten pastry right out of the oven and fainted, falling on the kitchen floor of her home in Paterson, New Jersey. She didn't allow water on the dinner table, either. When she was growing up, her cousins could never finish their meals because their parents had filled them up on water first. "Then they'd nag and nag those poor children to eat," she told us. She didn't allow soup, though she made an exception for Manhattan clam chowder, the only seafood beside shrimp and caviar that we'd willingly eat. We couldn't have pickles with our hamburgers because pickles and ice cream together were poison, and our meals always ended in ice cream, unless Mother insisted on fruit cocktail for our dessert. During summer months we couldn't order coleslaw, because of the mayonnaise, but there were no restrictions on chicken salad or egg salad.

"Why can we have chicken salad sandwiches? They're full of mayo, too."

"Is that what you want? Do you want me to say no chicken salad sandwiches, either? Because if that's what you want, that's what you'll get. I'm not joking, I'll do it."

"Ahh, Ma."

"Then don't argue."

We couldn't order tuna salad, regardless of the season.

"Your Aunt Ida practically died of tuna fish poisoning. It was touch and go, believe me."

"Ma, we hate fish!"

"Never you mind that! Just pay attention."

Father went downstairs once more to check the lobby and bar before dinner, while Peter and I went to our room to do homework and listen to the radio—*The Lone Ranger, The Green Hornet, Mr. Keene, Tracer of Lost Persons.* Our room was too small for a desk, so we lay on our beds to study. When the waiter returned with dinner, Mother knocked on our door. "Dee-nay ay servee." She and Aunt Mick had taken French lessons, leaving this residue.

The waiter rolled another room service table into the living room. Some evenings, there was an extra table to hold salads and desserts, depending on what we had ordered. Nearly every dessert except cake or pie arrived embedded in bowls of shaved ice, which took up room. The waiter covered the empty raviers and nappies with a clean tablecloth and wheeled the hors d'oeuvres table into the hall.

Laying a clean white napkin on the carpet, he crouched under the new table to lift out an aluminum heater. Three feet high and two and a half feet across, when filled with dinner for four or five, it was very heavy. Carefully, he placed it on the napkin on the floor. Gingerly, he opened the heater door, burning his fingers just the same. The pungent smell of burning jellied alcohol from a tiny can of Sterno on the heater's floor escaped into the room. The waiter took the metal covers off the dinner plates, put them on top of the heater, and took the heater away. If you touched the edge of a plate that had touched the side of the Sterno can on the trip upstairs, it would burn your fingers, though the food stayed tepid.

From the street, horns and brakes and the occasional meeting of bumper and fender rose to the fifteenth floor like an offering to the gods and made us feel all the cosier. On rainy nights, Peter and I leaned out the window and looked down on the shiny blacktop street until we were called back to finish our meal.

"How is the roast beef? Is it rare enough?"

"It's very good, Mom."

"It looks as if it has a lot of fat on it. I don't like it when they leave all that fat on. That's pure fat. I'll call Room Service and have them send up something else."

"Mom! I'm hungry. I won't eat the fat."

"Next time order steak instead. It's not so fatty. See, it's all yellow."

She tells about her uncle Nat, who loathes fat and who nagged Barney Greengrass, the Sturgeon King on Manhattan's West Side, to trim the fat off the corned beef until Greengrass, the old man himself, said, "Listen, Mister. I get up at four o'clock in the morning to get nice fat corned beef. Now get out!"

"Can we go to Barney Greengrass?"

Father says, "We have corned beef at the hotel just as good as Greengrass." We don't like the corned beef at the hotel. Mother says, "You like the corned beef and cabbage."

"That's different."

"No, it's not," she says. "You like the New England boiled dinner, too."

"It's not the same."

"It is," says Father. "It's the same corned beef and cabbage plus an onion and a carrot."

We squabble amiably. Father has heard the Barney Greengrass story many times, but both of them like retelling their favorite stories. Father's favorite is about the time he was fifteen, when he and his cousin Jesse took the trolley home after an evening in Chinatown. Under his arm, Jesse carried a box of the crystallized ginger both he and Father loved. Father's face always lit up as he told us, "This big Irish conductor said to Jesse, 'Hey, kid, what have you got in there?' Jesse holds out the box and says, 'Candy. Want some?' This big Irishman sticks his grimy paw in the box and grabs as much as he can—a big handful—and shoves it into his gob. Well, candied ginger, you know, it's very hot. Well, this big Irishman, he let out a yell and he jumped off the motorman's stool and Jesse and I jumped off the trolley—we'd already paid our nickel—and that big Irishman must have chased us five blocks." I love him when he's the jovial hotel manager whose job is to entertain and make welcome, not the one who's always checking bellmen's shoeshines, or mine.

The wind whistles through the windows, moaning down the long hotel corridor. Brakes squeal and horns blat outside. Peter looks over at the other room service table and pipes up. "The ice cream's melting."

"It's not melting. It's getting soft. Eat your vegetables."

"I like hard ice cream."

"Eat your vegetables or you won't get any ice cream."

After dinner, Father takes another turn downstairs, Mother calls Room Service to take away the table, and Peter and I go back to our bedroom. Until I was old enough for school and perhaps a year beyond, each night before I went to sleep I'd ask Mother or Grandma Esther for the roll I'd saved from dinner. I'd lie in bed and chew the dry roll in the semidarkness, the room lit only by the light shining through the bathroom door, cracked open as a night light. When I had finished all but the hard little end, I called out to Mother and handed the crust over. The roll was a special luxury, signifying, I suppose, that I had had enough.

*H*olidays are different for hotel families. New Year's Eve, Thanksgiving, and Christmas are when your father works hardest if you are a hotel kid. Father was up early Thanksgiving morning, checking on dinner reservations. He tried to find an empty room for Peter and me on the west side of the building, on a floor high enough so that we could see the Macy's parade on Broadway, a block to the west. If there were no rooms—people often rented them just to watch the parade—we'd go to the end of the corridor. Bridie came along to make sure we did not lean too far out the window. Friends from school came over to watch with us. They knew how lucky they were. Children on Broadway below, cold and battered on all sides, strained to see, able only to look straight up at the balloons' underbellies, while we were warm and comfortable, looking down on Mickey Mouse and Goofy. After an hour, our friends would go home to their dinners and we'd return to the suite for a light lunch. We didn't eat Thanksgiving dinner until five in the afternoon, when the midday diners in the Grill and the Tap Room had departed and the evening crowd hadn't yet arrived.

Father would come upstairs, exhausted. While he drank a highball, Mother called Chef, who took a new turkey out of the oven and carved the breast for us. It came upstairs on a platter taking up half the room service table, still warm, with thick-sliced, succulent shreds of skin hanging from the meat, surrounded by sauce boats of cranberry sauce, cranberry jelly, mayonnaise, and Thousand Island dressing. Platters of thin, hard-crusted Jewish rye bread allowed Peter and me to build ourselves jaw-breaking turkey sandwiches, smothered in near-candy-pink Thousand Island dressing. A plate under an aluminum cover held some of the day's stuffing for Mother to nibble on, and drumsticks for Peter and me to gnaw if we grew hungry later that evening, or else to share the next day with Bridie.

When Grandmother stayed with us, she would look at our turkey sandwiches and shake her head, sadly. "This is not Thanksgiving, Evelyn."

"It's what the boys want, Mom."

"Boys," Grandmother asked, "why don't you like a real Thanksgiving dinner?"

One year, Mother and Aunt Mick agreed that Peter and I needed a real Thanksgiving dinner in a real home. Grandmother took us to Aunt and Uncle's. She was delighted to be with her son and to see her hotel grandchildren sit at a real dinner table—one with a walnut veneer, place mats, and little silver dishes of olives and cashews. Mother stayed home, waiting for Father to come upstairs. Maybe, without us there, she met Father in the Tap Room. Maybe she didn't even have turkey. Free of children for the day and the traditions they require, she might have had a pair of Thanksgiving Scotches and a club sandwich.

At Aunt and Uncle's apartment, a maid served soup and asked us if we wanted light meat or dark. The breast was unevenly carved, some slices thick, some thin. The wings and legs looked as if they had first been sawed, then pulled off. There were brussels sprouts and mashed potatoes and two kinds of pie, but no Thousand Island dressing for the turkey, no ice-cream cake, and we had to sit up straight. "Wasn't that nice, boys?" Aunt Mick asked us at the conclusion of her real Thanksgiving dinner. "Very nice," we agreed, and it was, but we asked Mother not to send us back.

Peter and I didn't go from door to door on Halloween; no one did. Who had the nerve to trick or treat in Hell's Kitchen or Times Square? Mother sent a maid to Woolworth's to buy us costumes and candy corn. We were taken to Grey's Drugstore, where chorus boys and girls in Broadway shows bought their makeup. We'd buy sweet-smelling greasepaint with racist names like Comic Black or Chinaman and false hair to paste on our chins. Made up and costumed, we were entrusted to Smitty the Driver, a regular at the hack stand. He'd drive us to Mick and Cor's in his taxi and pick us up later, after we had bobbed for apples and eaten our fill of candy. Of course, we still had leftover makeup that we continued to use long after Halloween. Father wouldn't have let us wear it in the lobby; I suppose we slithered around the apartment in disguise.

Each Christmas and on his birthday as well, we bought Father a pair of black garters at the haberdashery on the corner. We shopped early because Father didn't wear garters in any color but black, and we were afraid the store might run out of stock. We bought jewelry for Mother from Aunt Dolly at the newsstand. Though she didn't ordinarily carry jewelry, Dolly could always sell for a half dollar or so a diamond pin or gold bracelet that Mother had sent downstairs the day before.

On Christmas morning, Peter and I opened presents under a tree in the living room. We didn't decorate our tree; we took one already tinseled from the stock of small trees bought for the maitre d's station in the Grill, the bandstand, and the bar. My earliest Christmas memory is of my heart exploding when I came out in my pajamas and found a red fire engine with real pedals under the tree. As I grew older, I asked for books—boys' series like Tom

Swift—always about the adventures of four or five chums, including a fat one, a foreigner, and a coward. A distant relative in California sent books every Christmas too young for us by four or five years; those left the apartment unopened. Our suite was too small for more than one bookcase in Esther's room. We had to throw out or give away an old book to make room for each new book we received. Like an orphan trying desperately to keep his siblings together, I schemed to keep my series intact, sacrificing individual titles where I had to.

For a few years when I could read and Peter hadn't yet learned to, it drove him wild. His face would take on a stubborn look as he tried to decipher the newspaper. He looked like Grandma Esther insisting that she wasn't hungry. Finally, he asked Mother to buy him books about dogs, his passion. She broke her rule about one book in, one book out and bought him half a dozen books by Albert Payson Terhune, the popular author of books about Lad of Sunnybank and other collies. Peter taught himself to read. Of course, once he learned, he had to scheme to keep his books together at Christmas, just as I did.

The Christmas tree, too, had to fit the dimensions of the living room—big enough for presents to fit under, small enough so that the waiter could wheel the dinner table in. But the tree in the lobby was at least twenty-five feet tall. To see the decorations on top, Peter and I got off at the mezzanine, walked over to the balustrade, and looked up. When school friends bragged about their trees, we brought them to the lobby. After they had agreed that our tree was bigger than theirs, we'd take them to the Coffee Shop to celebrate with a hot chocolate and then go to the Roxy. An even grander tree stood in the lobby there. After we had watched the movie, the tap dancers, and the comedians, the lights dimmed, and when they came back on, the audience gasped at a living crèche, center stage. Niches along the side walls were filled with chorus boys with white cotton beards and shepherds' crooks. The chorus girls wore halos. A giant pipe organ rose from the basement and, swelling in goose-flesh harmonies, joined Erno Rapee's Roxy Orchestra in "Adeste Fideles." We sang our hearts out.

On New Year's Eve, Mother and Father invited friends to cocktails and dinner. Mother told the night maid our bedtime. When she kissed us goodnight, we smelled whisky, cigarettes, and perfume. After they had all gone down to the Grill, we'd come out and explore the smoky living room, finishing the rest of the canapés: soggy bits of toast with caviar, stuffed eggs with crusty yellows, limp celery sticks lined with salty Roquefort. Our parents' bedroom window faced Times Square. We'd open it and shiver in the chilly air, listening to noisemakers, car horns, and people shouting. When the night maid put us to bed, we only pretended to sleep. We turned on the radio very softly and listened to the announcer describe the crowds just a few blocks away. By the time the radio went off at ten, we were no longer pretending.

On Saint Patrick's Day, Father and all the assistant managers wore green carnations. The hotel vibrated with excitement. The porters were all Irish. The floor maids and the supervising housekeepers were Irish. (Most of the city's hotel managers were Irish. I once asked Father why all but he had X for a middle initial, as in Francis Xavier Halloran.) Bridie took us to Saint Patrick's on Fifth Avenue and taught us how to light candles. That was fine with Mother; she always gave Bridie money to light candles to Saint Jude, the patron saint of lost causes. Peter and I loved Bridie, loved lighting candles at Saint Patrick's, and wanted to be Irish. Father, too, though not at ease with many people, seemed most comfortable with his Irish hotel counterparts. In a kind of tribute to Prohibition, repealed only a few years before, he'd boom at them, "Have a drink. It's just off the boat."

Once a year on Yom Kippur, Father went to an orthodox synagogue in a shabby building off Times Square. The men sat downstairs; the women were segregated upstairs. That would have killed it for Mother, even if she had been allowed to smoke and walk around when she got restless. Although she had grown up in a kosher household, she had little patience with the stringent requirements of religion. As a teenager, in a fit of temper, she had mixed up all her mother's meat and dairy dishes, which must be kept separate. Grandmother, divorced and hardworking, gratefully dropped the whole thing.

Mother went to the synagogue only once, at Peter's bar mitzvah. I wasn't bar mitzvahed; instead, I had gone to a Reform temple so liberal that Father said they served ham sandwiches on Yom Kippur. But Peter had his heart set on bar mitzvah presents and was willing to memorize whatever Hebrew prayers were necessary to get them.

After the rabbi said, "What a miracle that a boy brought up in the midst of wickedness—not only in Times Square, but in a hotel, in which it is best not to dwell on what particular worldlinesses occur—that a boy so brought up should find his way to righteousness," there was a lot of commotion up in the balcony in Mother's general vicinity. She never went to synagogue again. Once he had his presents, neither did Peter.

On Yom Kippur, Peter and I sometimes tried to fast, but toward the middle of the afternoon we'd walk to a nearby bakery and buy cupcakes piled high with icing. Tense with wickedness, we'd eat them on the way home. An hour later, I'd go to the synagogue so that I could walk home with Father. In the afternoon, the rabbi would raise money for the annual budget from those once-a-year

Jews. Congregants would rise and shout the amounts of their pledges. The synagogue was known as the Actor's Temple, and many of the names were well known. I would swivel around in my seat to see celebrities. "Toots Shor pledges two thousand dollars!" "That's all, Toots?" the rabbi would shout back. "Can't you do better than that!"

I'd walk Father home through twilit Times Square, the electric signs reflecting on the asphalt streets in the gathering dark. I pointed out my favorite movie theaters and orange drink stands, the Planter's Peanut store where I waved to Mr. Peanut in his top hat and peanut-shell suit. When we arrived home, Mother came out to greet us very differently from the matter-of-fact way she called out from her bedroom other evenings. She gently helped father off with his coat. In the living room, a table was waiting. Gefilte fish, matzoh ball soup, to be reheated on a hot plate, and other traditional Jewish dishes would be ready for us, delivered in paper containers from a nearby delicatessen, the only meal all year that wasn't sent upstairs from Room Service.

four

The streets in front of the Taft, though less crowded than today, were noisier. Cars were so few that before 1931, they could park at the curb in Times Square. You could just pull up alongside the Palace Theater, say, or the Brill Building, turn off the ignition, and go about your business. But every other way to get around, except walking, involved metal moving against metal. Subway lines under Sixth Avenue, Seventh, Broadway, and Eighth each made their own contribution to the noisy pulse of the streets, and trolleys ran up and down Seventh Avenue. In fact, photographs taken in 1915 by engineers planning to put in the subway show a five-story red brick building on the site of the Taft; it was a New York Railways car barn.

There was noise overhead, too. The Sixth Avenue Elevated crossed Fifty-third Street to meet the Ninth Avenue El and continue north. Nothing grinds, squeals, and clatters louder than an el. Holding onto Bridie's hand, walking under the tracks as a train passed overhead, our teeth shook.

In the spring, people walked slowly and stopped to smile at us. In the fall, they moved briskly, their shoulders hunched against the wind. Then we lingered over the subway gratings for the comfort of the warm, cindery air that rose from the tracks. On Seventh Avenue, a whole spectrum of smells assaulted our young nostrils. Grass and manure surrounded us whenever Peter stopped to feed the horses standing dazedly at the curb between the shafts of their wagons. Stale beer hung in a malty envelope outside the saloon on Fifty-third Street. We passed a Chinese restaurant that closed and reopened under new management every few years, as languidly as a silk fan. Old apartment houses on the corners exhaled decades of dust. Walking by their lobbies was like passing King Tut's tomb with the door open. They were inhabited by retired schoolteachers, violin repairmen working out of their apartments, and city workers with old-fashioned New York accents. The buildings' original facades were hidden behind fake white tile or fake black marble, fronting bars, dry cleaners, candy stores.

If we saw Brian rolling down the green awning over his Irish grocery, we'd wave and he'd wave back. He was very fond of Grandma Esther. Occasionally she'd buy something from him for friendship's sake; it would stay a few days in a refrigerator we kept in the extra bathroom adjoining the living room; then it would grow hard or soft or moldy, and would be thrown out.

At every corner, shoeshine boys snapped their cloths and called out to us. Bridie would stop in front of a boy only a few years older than we and carefully supervise our shine, while we looked down on his head and our shoes, incuriously. When he finished, he'd look up at Bridie for her money, as uninterested in us as we were in him.

In Central Park, we visited a smelly pond that held a few lethargic ducks and a flock of crabby geese. At the carousel, Peter begged to ride the wooden horses, but he was always furious by the end of the ride. His arms weren't long enough to reach the brass ring that would entitle him to a free ride.

Returning home on Sixth Avenue, we hurried past clumps of men in front of employment agencies—just storefronts whose doors and windows were pasted over with handwritten notices of low-paying jobs. Men in shabby jackets or threadbare coats paid no attention to us but made me uncomfortable all the same. What really interested me was a fish store with a turtle shell in the window. The shell was about two feet across and two and a half feet long. I was not convinced that the turtle wasn't alive—it might be very slow or sleeping—but I was never allowed to watch it long enough to find out. Bridie would yank my arm and hurry us back to the Taft. One afternoon, I ran away and hid when she called to Peter and me that we were going home. I waited at corners for lights to turn green. I didn't talk to strangers. I tried to look purposeful, so that a policeman wouldn't think I was lost. I stopped in front of the fish store long enough to be sure that the turtle was not slow or sleeping but incontrovertibly dead. Despite a spanking from Bridie, I went to bed that night very satisfied with myself. I can still see that turtle shell. I can see the men in their threadbare coats, too.

On rainy days and weekends, Bridie would take us to the movies. There were at least twenty-five theaters within eight blocks of the hotel. Many of the great legitimate theaters—the New Amsterdam on Forty-second Street, the Ziegfeld on Fifty-fourth—had been turned into second-run houses that showed a cowboy movie, a gangster movie, a comedy short, a chapter from a serial, and a newsreel, all for a dime. Bridie would buy us candy and watch the movie with us, never taking her eyes from the screen as she slapped our hands if we picked our noses. On our way home, we stopped to study the framed eight-by-ten photos outside the other theaters. During the Depression, some Times Square theaters turned to burlesque. We didn't always know the difference between the photos of movie stars and those that showed wet-lipped exotic beauties, their hands on pasty-covered nipples, until Bridie yanked us sharply on.

We went to the great movie palaces, too. Three, running east to west between Fiftieth and Fifty-first Streets, were the Radio City Music Hall on Sixth Avenue, the Roxy next door on Seventh, and the Capitol on Broadway. Both Radio City and the Roxy were the brainchildren of S. L. Rothafel, whose nickname was Roxy. The Roxy had the Gae Foster Girls, clones of the Radio City Rockettes. All three, as well as the Paramount a few streets down, showed only one movie but had stage shows and bands as well. There we saw the final days of acts that had toured America unchanged for years. They were short and uncomplicated, staying vivid in the memory for the year or more that might pass between visits. A drunk takes five minutes to stagger up the ladder to a high diving board placed over a prop swimming pool. Slipping, missing his footing, lurching from side to side, he finally reaches the tip of the board, only to topple backward the board's length and plummet down the ladder head first, until miraculously, before we have time to gasp, he faces us at the bottom, his feet firmly planted on the stage, waiting for our applause.

We loved Peg Leg Bates, a genius tap dancer who, with just one leg of flesh and bone, blazed on the stage. We hated to watch the chorus girls steady themselves in a line, on top of medicine balls three feet high. We could see the tension on their faces as they balanced themselves, trying to move the balls forward and back in formation, with tiny skipping motions. They were right to be scared; there was usually at least one who would fall and have to be carried off the stage behind the other girls, still teetering, still in line.

When the Roxy opened each afternoon, the usher corps, 125 young men in dress blues, stood at attention in the lobby through inspection by the usher captain, then performed close-order drill. In late afternoon, the evening ushers, resplendent in white mess jackets trimmed with gold braid, replaced the blue-uniformed daytime corps. If we could not arrive early enough for the opening inspection, next best was watching the changing of the guard at dusk.

Originally, an entrance to the Roxy Theater was planned from within our lobby. That never came to pass. The theater box office, though, was just steps south of the Taft Coffee Shop. One rainy afternoon, a substitute maid assigned to take us to the movies hurried us from our marquee to theirs—a two-second dash. The theater was crowded, probably because of the weather. We ascended the grand staircase to the promenade level and then up to the balcony, beyond which curving stairs led to the tower foyer. We probably wanted to climb there so that we could look down on the lobby, but there is no reason to assume that a maid, choosing the Roxy because it was nearest theater, would have climbed four flights of stairs just to see a movie. The movie was *The Bride of Franken-stein*. I was six and Peter was five. When we saw the monster, we started to scream. We screamed and screamed. When it became clear that nothing likely to happen on the screen was going to stop us, the maid led us to the art moderne lounge outside the rest rooms. They served tea there. We sat outside the ladies room, sobbing for some time, then sniffling, then waiting for the movie to finish and the stage show to begin, then whining and making the maid ask the usher whether the stage show had started. Perhaps because we pestered him so, the usher jumped the gun just slightly, motioning us to follow him, though the movie was not quite over. As we went back to our seats, we saw the monster catapulted into a boiling cauldron in the burning castle of Baron von Frankenstein. We screamed and screamed and screamed.

When I was eight and in the third grade, Mother let me walk to school without Bridie. None of the other children at P.S. 69 had maids or anyone else to walk them to school, and I didn't want anyone, either. I had been pestering Mother for a long time, and she knew I could not be walked to school indefinitely. But she was nervous. "You used to daydream so, I didn't know if you'd wait for the light or get lost or lose Peter or what." She assigned a porter to follow me the first day to make sure I could manage by myself. She told me later he had reassured her that I was careful crossing streets and watched out for Peter, as I was supposed to. "But he said you weaved back and forth all over the place, from the curb to the buildings and back to the curb. He worried about you—he said you didn't seem able to walk a straight line."

On the far side of Fifty-first Street, across from the Taft, we'd first pass the Hotel Victoria. Though it was slightly more expensive than the Taft (during the Depression, perhaps fifty cents or a dollar a night more), Peter and I had learned to say at an early age that they took our overflow—that is, when we were fully booked and could not honor reservations or accommodate walk-ins, our front office would send disappointed guests across the street. At Fifty-third Street, we'd stop at the tiny mom-and-pop candy store for bubble gum. Uncle Al and Aunt Dolly didn't carry bubble gum or the cards that came with the gum, currency at school.

Except for a few actors' kids, my school gathered most of its student body from San Juan Hill and Hell's Kitchen, a few blocks west, neighborhoods that had enjoyed a terrible reputation for over a century. My closest friend in the third grade, Charley Ellis, lived in Hell's Kitchen. He sometimes hitched rides on the backs of trolley cars. He insisted that I stay on the sidewalk. Looking at me dubiously out of pale blue eyes set flatly in his face, he said, "You'd get yourself killed." Charley loved setting false alarms, and each morning, when we met in front of school, he told me about the fire engines he had summoned. He also described fires he saw on the way to school, in which dozens of people died, usually throwing themselves off the roof with their hair burning in a fiery comet tail behind. After school, we walked back to the Taft. At the Hotel Victoria, he'd dart from my side into the bar. I'd wait until he rushed out, a handful of pretzels or potato chips in his grasp, shouting goodbye as he ran down Seventh Avenue. Not many maids could have run fast enough to walk Charley Ellis home from school.

I often invited him home with me for lunch. Most of our classmates lived in cold-water flats "on the relief" and ate a free lunch provided by the school. Mother encouraged us to bring them over for a good hot meal. Sometimes Peter invited his best friends, Angelo and Mario, brothers who were in the same grade, though one was two years older than the other. They walked through the lobby so close that their shoulders touched. They came upstairs, ate silently, and left. I told Peter they were scared stiff. Charley wasn't afraid of anything. Wolfing down his lunch, he'd tell us about the meals at his house—great ribs of beef and his mother's suety Yorkshire pudding. His parents were English. His father had resigned from the Cunard Line some years previously by neglecting to reboard when his ship returned to Southhampton. Charley was a wonderful raconteur. I still remember his story about pouring ink in the black bean soup at the school's free lunch. Charley said the soup was so bad that no one who ate it could tell what he had done.

Charley wasn't the toughest kid in the third grade, but he was the toughest kid who was my friend. The toughest kid in the third grade, in the whole school, probably, was Eugene, who had recently moved to New York from West Virginia. He chewed tobacco. He was nearly fourteen. In those days, students who had not satisfactorily completed the year's work were held back to repeat it. Whenever I hear self-righteous parents complain about social promotion—the passing of children regardless of their academic achievement—I remember the young men and women in my third-grade classroom, waiting until they were old enough for working papers. People who object to social promotion should have to repeat the third grade with Eugene.

When Peter was in the second grade, he was assigned a classmate who had recently come out second best in a knife fight and had lost a lot of blood. If Peter saw the boy start to faint, he was to raise his hand and get the teacher's attention immediately. The whole school had a reputation for toughness. According to the word around the halls, because there were so few children in the neighborhood, our school accepted kids rejected as incorrigible by other schools in the city.

A series of articles on New York City's schools that appeared in the *New York Tribune* in 1898 confirmed this. In the 1870s, according to the reporter, "there was a somewhat undesirable class of pupils. Boys who had been refused admission into other schools, or had been dropped for bad behavior, came here." He went on: "For some years after the school building was erected pigs, chickens and goats were more numerous in Fifty-fourth-st than school children were. . . . It is unfortunate that the usefulness of such a school as Grammar School 69 in Fifty-fourth-st near Sixth-avenue is impaired by an inadequate building." The building grew nearly forty years older before Peter and I attended but remained unchanged and inadequate. The playground was covered in cement. For fear of injury to the students, playground exercise was limited to walking in a circle—"Slowly, boys! Slowly!"— for fifteen minutes each morning, the boys clockwise, the girls, in a smaller circle, counterclockwise. In the bathroom adjoining the cement playground, flimsy toilet seats were constructed over a trough filled with running water.

We were all afraid of falling in. Another trough served as a urinal. The combined effect of boys daydreaming while urinating, pushing each other while urinating, and showing off how far they could urinate made the floor unspeakable.

The best-behaved children in school were the sons and daughters of Chinese waiters and restaurant owners. For years afterward, Peter and I would see them working in Chinese restaurants around town. The next best behaved was me. I was polite, did my homework, and didn't know what a prize I was. I thought that teachers didn't like me—I was so used to being treated like the boss's son that I had no way of knowing how people behaved toward children to whose fathers they were not beholden.

When we returned at three from school, with our homework under our arms and the street already in blue shadow, a doorman spun the revolving door for Peter and me and we'd swing into the warm, welcoming lobby. The bronze fixtures lent a cheerful orange glow to winter afternoons. We'd check the newsstand for any new comic books and go down to the pantry to get an eclair.

A month before Christmas 1937, Bridie showed up for work red-eyed and crying. The maids and housemen and some of the elevator men were going out on strike the next day. Peter and I didn't know what that meant. She explained that instead of cleaning rooms and taking care of us, she would be marching in front of the hotel. Would she have to do it in her uniform? we wanted to know. No, she'd dress in her regular clothes. Would she wear an overcoat? We knew we were half-frozen when we came back from school. Yes, she'd wear her warmest coat and a scarf and a hat and mittens. We'll come down and keep you company, we promised.

As it turned out, that was a promise we didn't keep. Mother wouldn't let us leave the hotel, not even to go to school. She was afraid pickets would frighten us, curse us, maybe even hurt us. She might have been right. The elevator union had already made use of flying squads elsewhere—strong-arms organized to protect striking workers as they walked off their jobs. But the strong-arms soon gained a reputation for threatening operators who had not yet decided to strike. Sometimes men were hurt. Our elevator men and housemen—those who didn't walk off their jobs, as well as the scabs hired to replace those who did—slept on cots set up in the Village Room, behind the bar. Charley Drew didn't sing naughty songs that week. A hotel spokesman (probably Father) said, "No inconvenience was experienced by the hotel's two thousand guests."

I don't believe we had two thousand guests. Most of the hotels in New York then were in receivership. Six months before, the Taft had been sold to its bondholders for $3 million, as low as the court would allow the price to go. (It had cost $10 million to build ten years before that.) The Taft's profit that year was $24,906—for the effort of a thousand men and women. The bondholders said the current manager would continue, but we didn't know for how long.

The 25 percent increase the employees demanded was less than two dollars to a maid or houseman on a weekly salary of seven dollars. Peter and I were embarrassed that Father, who rarely said no to us, refused our friends in the hotel. We did not know that even a fifty-cent-a-week raise would have put the hotel back in the red.

Father explained that seven dollars a week was better than it sounded when you took tips and free meals into account. When he was young, he told us, bellmen and porters paid hotels. Just like concessions, they rented the right to work in the hotel, for tips. That didn't sound fair to us, though we knew that free meals were important. Not only were we often reminded—"Do you know how much those shrimp you're inhaling would cost if we had to pay for them?"—but we saw hard times whenever we went out. We fed the pigeons and ducks in the park with stale rolls until we were approached by two boys our own age, asking for one of the rolls we were holding out to the birds. We thought they wanted to feed the birds, too. The boy who took the roll I handed him broke off a small piece with his teeth. The roll was so old and hard he could not have bitten off more. We handed the other rolls to the boys and left. After that, we felt so bad that we stopped bringing rolls to the birds. Of course, we should have brought more rolls, rather than none, but reality outside the comfortable cocoon of the hotel embarrassed us.

New York, which had always been the gateway for newcomers, may have suffered a greater sense of betrayal by the Depression than other parts of the country lacking New York's immigrant optimism. It is hard for a society that has developed the ability to walk past people living in cardboard boxes to understand how the Depression shamed and frightened everyone. What our school friends on the relief could have shown us, if they wanted to, would have cracked us open like a pair of two-minute eggs. All over the city, there were bread lines and soup kitchens of which we were only dimly aware. They served eighty-five thousand meals a day in 1932, when the sous-chef was puréeing vegetables for Peter. Still, city hospitals more than once reported starvation as a cause of death. An emergency committee raised millions of dollars to provide jobs, but they could keep only a few thousand people employed, and then only for thirty weeks. The city borrowed money to keep men working—three days a week at first, then two, then the money ran out. New York City residents were allowed to stay in city shelters for five nights, transients for only one, before they had to move on, God knows where.

After eight days, the strikers returned to their jobs, with a dollar raise but without the closed shop or paid vacations they also wanted. Peter and I were afraid Bridie or other friends at the hotel would be angry or blame us because Father hadn't given them what they wanted. But a hotel is like a ship: you've got to get along or get off.

Sensitivity and father-son bonding weren't high priorities during the Depression, but Father did take me out once for the afternoon, and I understood him better at the end of the day, though he was unaware of that. Peter had gone out to a classmate's birthday party. Father came upstairs just before noon, wearing his overcoat. "You like Chinese food, don't you?" he asked.

"Mom hates Chinese."

"Just us."

We went to a side-street restaurant off Sixth Avenue and had glutinous chop suey, glutinous sweet-and-sour pork, fried noodles, and fortune cookies from a cellophane pack. I sat up straight and told him about school, about homework, about my Chinese classmates. I thought gleefully of Peter stuck at some dumb birthday party. After lunch, walking back to the Taft, Father called to me as I started to walk down West Forty-fifth Street. I turned and saw him waiting for me on the corner. I went back and we walked in silence to Forty-sixth Street and up to Seventh Avenue. Though I searched both sides of Forty-sixth Street for the surprise he had in mind—which would have made two surprises in one day—we walked without incident until we got home. He nodded to the doorman. At the elevators, we entered an empty car, the starter smoothly put his body in front of the gate and directed guests to the next car, the doors closed, and we rose silently to the fifteenth floor.

I asked Mother about Forty-sixth Street and she explained that there had been nothing to see there; it was the Hotel Knickerbocker on Forty-fifth Street that Father was avoiding. If you think you've heard of it, you're probably confusing it with the famous turn-of-the-century Hotel Knickerbocker on Forty-second Street. Our Knickerbocker was only a small side-street hotel, across from Texas Guinan's speakeasy, but Mother spoke of it with great affection. (A bar in the lobby, called the Peppermint Lounge, achieved a brief spasm of fame thirty-five years later, when Killer Joe Piro taught New York society the twist there.) Father had lost it in the first year of the Depression.

Father's father had financed the initial payments for the hotel in the mid-twenties for him and for his cousin Oscar. By 1930, unable to keep up the payments, he and

Oscar had to return the hotel to the bank. Empty rooms, empty restaurant tables, slow pay, meetings ending in long faces, layoffs, more layoffs, then the closing, an anti-climax everyone had seen coming for months. When it was finally over, Father and Mother and I moved into a tiny apartment, a second baby, Peter, soon to be on the way. Father and Mother blamed the Depression; Mother blamed Cousin Oscar, too, who had compounded his injury by dying young, leaving a baby and a young widow. Father was out of work for a year, not sure that times would ever get better, before he was hired by the new owners of the Taft as a consultant. The hotel had been about to fall into receivership when its major creditor took it over. My father delivered a report so detailed and thorough that he was offered the managership. His sigh of relief must have shaken Manhattan's granite schist. He brought with him as many of the men who had worked for him at the Knickerbocker as he could: Charlie, Smitty, Tony, the ones who had known me "since before I was born."

Father was at work on the mezzanine long before his clerks arrived in the morning and long after they picked up their purses and went home for the night. At the top of a pyramid that must have seemed insurmountable to a Cuban dishwasher working downstairs in the steamy kitchen, Father, for thirty-three years, feared losing his job. Firing and being fired were always on his mind. When I was nine, he looked down at my shoes and irritably remarked that if someone who worked for him couldn't tie his shoelaces neater than that, he would have been fired.

When Peter and I walked down the corridor, maids shrank back against the wall. They were supposed to. According to Father's manual, "Employees will always give preference to guests in entering elevators, passing in corridors, in service at cashier's counters, etc. throughout the building." Father published thousands of rules in the hotel's operating manual. The reasons for some were clear. "People who claim they have lost their key or left it in the room and request admittance will politely be sent to the Front Office Desk." Others were less so. "Employees will not patronize the restaurants in the hotel." "Do not return to visit the building after your working hours." I suppose he worried about the potential for collusion, a steak slipped to a pal or some other larceny. A hotel is a building full of people and pillows, steaks and silverware, and everything in it can walk or be carried out. If he let his guard slip, housemen would steal paint or monkey wrenches; bartenders would steal bottles of Scotch, or worse, sneak in their own stock so they could pocket the customer's money without affecting the inventory. Cooks stole live lobsters, secreting them God knows where. Father checked the Grill a few times a night to see if there was a line at the door while empty tables were available (a sure sign of extortion *maître d'hôtel*). Captains put elderly couples next to the bandstand to encourage tips for a table farther away and sat young couples far from the band in order to get tips for tables closer to the dance floor. For New Year's Eve, Father assigned the room clerks, up in the lobby, to take Grill Room reservations. The room clerks would be home New Year's Eve and so had no way to extort bribes for tables.

Some rules seemed miserly: "Employees who bring food for their meals into the hotel will not use hotel linens and utensils such as spoons, knives, forks, china, coffee and tea pots, salt and pepper shakers." He even had a rule about the manuals: "You may take this manual home with you to read, but if you do so, you must bring it back to work with you within a few days, since it must be kept available in your locker during working hours."

Many employees did not speak English, but Father understood them. His favorite maxims were "Never fire a chef for stealing unless you can find one who doesn't steal" and "In empty restaurants, the waiters get depressed and the service is terrible." A maid told me, "We used to throw empty bottles down the incinerator. We knew we shouldn't—it said so on the incinerator and the supervisors always told us not to, but it was too far to carry them back where they were supposed to go. Your father called a meeting of all us maids. He didn't say a word. The men who cleaned out the incinerator got up instead and showed us the cuts they got from glass falling down on them and from handling broken glass. None of us dropped bottles down after that."

To those who failed to follow his rules he must have seemed gifted with supernatural powers. In the days before blinking message lights on room phones, a copy of each message was placed in the room slot at the mail desk and another was handed in a sheaf to a bellman to distribute under guest doors. One morning, running behind schedule, a bellman tore up the remaining dozen messages he had been given and tossed them out the window. They wafted on updrafts and downdrafts along the outside of the building until they floated into our open living room window. Father scooped up the scraps of paper and went out, slamming the apartment door behind him. To that terrified bellman, he must have seemed in league with the devil.

The man who could write three pages on what to do if a dissatisfied guest wanted a different room ("Change the room number on the rack slip by circling the old number and drawing a line down to open space on bottom. . . . Fill out a Rooming Slip in triplicate. . . .") came upstairs at the end of the day to find his children wrestling on his bed. School books and comic books lay on the floor or on the sofa, on our bed or on his. Our shirttails hung out. Our noses ran. He often seemed surprised to see us there. Mother explained, "Most men take the train or the subway home. They have time to get over their day. Aunt Sarah always made sure Moe had an apple to eat on the bus so he wouldn't walk in hungry and irritable."

"Couldn't Father eat an apple?"

"Don't be silly. He couldn't eat an apple on the elevator."

While Father devised rules for everything, Mother resented any rule but her own, developing into a kind of deeply authoritarian anarchist. When a plumber or electrician came upstairs to change a faucet or replace a frayed wire, she'd tell him to fix himself a drink. Father, whose manual featured four pages on not drinking while on duty, told her how many rules she was breaking. "Oh, Alfred." Employees must have thought of her the way one would a pet Kodiak bear—friendly but so powerful you could never relax in its presence.

The men and women who worked in the hotel were mainly immigrants. Europeans tended in those days to be what Americans would consider overrespectful; those who had trained in Berlin or Hamburg, like many at the Taft, would have deferred to authority even if they had come over first class on the *Bremerhaven*. Barely escaping with their lives from the menace of totalitarian bullies, their first impulse, always, was to tremble. Once I asked a cashier to change a five-dollar bill. Nervously she counted out the money. As she handed it to me, she said, "Thank you, please, Mr. Sir."

When maids made way for us in the corridors, placing their palms against the wall, they looked just like Fay Wray in *King Kong*. But we weren't giant gorillas; we were just a couple of little kids. We never forgot that the deference everyone paid us was borrowed from Father. Mother, on the other hand, didn't mind if it was borrowed, just so long as it was paid. It wasn't surprising that she grew increasingly imperious on a steady, heady diet of servility. She claimed she helped Father maintain the standard of excellence that was his job and our livelihood. But Father, who sometimes emptied ashtrays in the living room while his guests were holding their cigarettes over them, needed no help making sure the Taft was flawlessly run.

Something within wouldn't let her say "All right, okay, good enough." Peter, age twelve, looked up from his chocolate ice cream and slammed his spoon down on the tablecloth, exclaiming, "This is ice-cold!" I burst into laughter. "Ice-cold" was one of her favorite expressions. "Ice-cold, no taste at all, too tough to cut, pure salt, nothing but fat, swimming in butter, bitter as gall, not fit for a dog." What made it worse was how complicated her orders were. "A club sandwich on white toast, but leave out the third slice of toast. And toast the bread twice, do you understand? Crisp. Do you understand? Crisp, crisp, crisp. But not burned."

Father explained that when we ordered something not on the menu or required a complicated substitution, we strained the ability of the room service order taker, who was generally too incompetent to be trusted with a waiter's station of his own. That was why it said "No substitutions, please" at the bottom of the menu. The order takers were terrified of Mother and tried desperately to please, but giving her what she wanted must have seemed to them like memorizing random sounds in some nightmare psychology test, where the penalty for failure might be losing your job. She ordered sauerkraut. It came enriched with butter and jauntily garnished with parsley. She sent it back downstairs and called Room Service. She explained that she liked sauerkraut plain, no butter, no parsley, nothing fancy. "Do you understand? Plain. Simple. *Just the way it comes from the can.*" A waiter arrived no more than four minutes later with a tray covered by a stiff, starched napkin. Underneath, there was a cold, open can of sauerkraut.

When she complained about her dinner, the waiter would look down at his feet, holding his napkin in his big red hands. If he offered to bring another portion in just a minute or substitute something she might prefer, she'd say it would take too long or would decide when it arrived that she was no longer hungry. When she yelled at a waiter, our cheeks grew hot with shame. We wanted to run out of the room, but like the unlucky waiter, we had to stay and take it. Harry the Waiter cried once when she yelled at him for some room service blunder. We burst into tears, too. After he left, we told her the waiters spit in her food.

Before Monsieur Martin, the chef, formidable, mustachioed, and red-faced, returned to France, he came upstairs to say goodbye. Mother told us she started to cry and told him she was sorry she had been so difficult. Then his eyes filled and he said, "No, no! You were right." Then they both cried.

The only employee Mother never yelled at was Robbins the Package Boy. His vacant pale blue eyes and willingness to do whatever he was told put him above criticism or even impatience. If she had asked him to wait on line for two days to pick up tickets for an audience with the Pope, he would have listened carefully, nodding, and, when she was finished, taken from his uniform pocket a little stub of pencil to write down the address. She spoke to Robbins gently, but no one else could expect to escape her temper.

Once, she fired the Coffee Shop manager. "She was fresh!" Mother claimed indignantly, a word she used to describe anything from simple disagreement to insurgency. She might have thought Father liked the manager, young and slim, too much. She might have been right. Still, Mother didn't work at the Taft; she couldn't fire anyone. When Father went down to the Coffee Shop to apologize and avert a union action, she grew even angrier. It was not so much that she couldn't grasp reality—she knew she couldn't fire anyone—it was more that she dismissed it as if it were just another clumsy waiter. Her argument of choice was exasperation. "Oh, Alfred!" was her favorite response to Father's careful logic.

Once, Mother was in the hospital, scheduled for a serious operation. Father was crying; Peter and I were sure she would die. That morning, during the preliminaries, she received an anesthetic that left her groggy. Peter and Father and I sat nervously in her room while she called the anesthesiologist. She told him she had not liked the anesthetic and asked what he would recommend in its place. He came up with an alternative that he promised she would find satisfactory. Peter turned and whispered, as much to comfort himself as me, "It'll be okay. She's sending back the anesthetic." He was right. The operation was a success. She was fine.

Mother inherited her temper from her father. It was he who began what we all called the "Aronsohn look." Grandfather Harry had it most intensely, then our Uncle Nat, his youngest brother. Even Uncle Corny, Harry's mild-mannered son, could, when crossed, flash you an angry stare from under his prominent prefrontal lobes that would freeze your blood.

When he came to America, Grandfather Harry worked in a Paterson silk mill for seven dollars a week. He fell in love with Esther, also working in Paterson, and pursued her relentlessly. Esther had come to America from Russia. When her father died, leaving her with a stepmother who favored her own children, she set out with an uncle for the U.S., was turned back at the Russian border twice, finally arrived in Hamburg without her uncle, sailed to America at the age of fourteen, moved in with cousins on the Lower East Side, left when another uncle "got fresh," and moved to Paterson and the Arrow Shirt Company. "The hardest part of the shirt is the collar. They wouldn't let anybody but me touch the collars."

Grandfather Harry was homely, she said, a man of intense, irresistible charm. He made money, bought a small silk mill, then a large one, then made a fortune in the stock market. Money ruined him. He took a mistress, "a humpbacked Irish washerwoman," said Grandmother, still bitter. After he failed to come home one night, she climbed the stairs to their roof and opened his pigeon coops. None of the homing birds returned, she said, as if the birds confirmed her opinion of the man. She divorced him, the first person any of her friends had ever known who got divorced. In fact, she was the only person besides Gloria Swanson they had ever even heard of getting a divorce. Harry married twice more, garnered more dollars and women. His last wife, twenty years younger than he, caught him cheating. She kept the Park Avenue apartment. He lost whatever money remained in the crash of '29.

When Harry was broke, with no one to take care of him, Mother persuaded Father to give him a tiny room with a toilet and a sink on the eleventh floor. The bath was down the hall, for the use of the smallest, cheapest rooms. He shared his room with a canary, all that was left from his last marriage.

Mother stayed angry all her life over the scandal of her parents' divorce. His mistress's children, she told us, were driven to school in a Rolls-Royce while she and her brother, Corny, walked. She explained that when alimony wasn't enough to get them through the month she had to put on torn clothes to go to her father's house to ask for more money. She looked back on her youth as a time bitter as gall, ice-cold, not fit for a dog. "You'll never see me at his funeral," she used to say.

She refused to see him, except once a year. On his birthday or a date close to it, when she was sure Esther wouldn't be there, she'd invite him to our suite for lunch. She fussed over the menu, ordering special smoked salmon, and sent someone to Dunhill's to pick up a pair of his favorite cigars. He enjoyed his lunch and his cigar, sitting luxuriously back in his chair, telling funny stories, the second cigar sticking out of his breast pocket for later. When lunch was over, he went back to his room on the eleventh floor. Mother would tell us again how she had never met anyone who wasn't charmed by his extravagances and his generosity, though it clearly had not focused on her. Esther agreed. "He was always a sport," she said. "Stephen, always be a sport. Like your grandfather, may he rot in hell."

When she took her imperious ways outside the hotel, Mother found herself impotent—perhaps that was why she went out so rarely. Dressed to go out, she could be startlingly handsome. We could tell that she was getting ready to go when we saw her take a smudged tin of mascara from the medicine cabinet above her sink and spit in it. She applied it to her lashes, squinting and swearing. Around her neck, she wrapped an old sable, its teeth angrily biting its tail. She put on a big, feathered hat that framed her face, or a small one with a veil, which she lifted frequently to puff on her cigarette. If she was going farther than two long east-west blocks or four short north-south ones, she'd call the doorman and he'd tell Smitty at the hack stand to hang around, Mrs. Lewis was going out.

She was a nervous walker, not taking her eyes from the pavement for fear she would fall. If we were with her and she wanted to say something, she'd take our arm, stop in the middle of the sidewalk, and not move on until she had finished what she wanted to say. In her purse she carried smelling salts in a small glass vial covered with mesh to protect her fingers if she felt faint and had to crush the glass. She had once suffered an allergic reaction to a bee sting and her doctor recommended that she keep a little brandy nearby. She could die if she were stung again, she told us. The brandy was always in her purse, though bees were few on Fifty-first Street. She worried about low blood sugar, too, and carried gumdrops that she greedily chewed if she felt weak or shaky. Peter and I never ate the gumdrops. After a few days in her purse, they were unbearably saturated with the smell of perfume. Although I grew dubious about her low blood sugar as I got older—she had all sorts of notions, convictions, and diseases that no one but she had ever heard of (I remember, for example, a "dropped stomach")—I sometimes get shaky, too. When I do, I grab for something sweet.

When I needed a new suit, which mother couldn't order over the phone or trust Bridie to pick out, she took me shopping. After we had selected a suit, the salesman called the alterations man, and he stood me on the podium. When he started chalking the jacket cuffs, Mother interrupted him. "That shoulder's all wrong. See." She lifted the shoulder pad as he was pinning it, so that he had to take his hand away or pierce her. "And his jackets always wrinkle back here. *Stand up straight!*" (The alterations man and I both stood straighter.) A week later, when Robbins brought the suit upstairs, Mother was unhappy with the alterations. We went out again, the second time in ten days. I knew the store was in trouble. Sure enough, meeting with the salesman and the alterations man, she segued seamlessly from the suit's flaws to their own.

"How long have you been doing this? Didn't anyone teach you how a shoulder should look?"

The store manager came over. "Mr. Donatello, what seems to be the problem?"

"Mr. Damico told me to take in the shoulder here and the back here."

Mother interrupted, grabbing the back of the jacket, shaking me like a terrier shakes a rat. "Do you see this *hump?*"

"Mrs. Lewis—"

"Do you?"

"Mr. Donatello. Make out a credit slip. Take the suit back."

"I'm certainly not coming back here!" Mother said angrily. "We'd appreciate that, Madam," someone called after us, as she dragged me, skipping and bobbing in her wake, past Neckties, Gloves, and Socks.

Many of the men and women who worked at the hotel enjoyed her warmth and the generous spirit that rose above her demanding nature. She asked housekeepers about their husbands, and dried-up chambermaids about their sex lives, presumably in some other time or country. She used sign language of her own to learn how many children the Romanian furniture refinisher, in this country for only a month, had and how many were boys. She charmed my friends, too, treating them as if she were unaware that they were children. (Perhaps, distracted, she was unaware.) "Oh, Bobby, good to see you," she'd say to a classmate of Peter's. She'd laugh and put her hand to her forehead. "I have such a hangover," she'd explain. "I've got to learn not to drink after dinner."

For a few years, both my grandfathers and Grandma Esther lived within a few hundred yards of us and one another, either vertically or horizontally. Although they lived on different floors, Mother was terrified that Harry and Esther would meet in an elevator or the lobby. Esther had not spoken to Harry in forty years. Mother needn't have worried; Harry rarely left his room. Though nominally an insurance agent, thanks to a friend who allowed him to try to sell policies on straight commission, his only prospects were friends who had lost all their money, too.

Father's father, Grandfather Morris, stayed at the hotel after Grandmother Elizabeth, a portly woman who called him "Mister," died. He moved out of his large apartment on the West Side into a suite at the other end of the fifteenth floor. He brought as much of his old-fashioned furniture as he could install in two hotel rooms. On top of every table he placed a porcelain dish filled with hard candies with liquid centers, wrapped in lovely colored foils. Peter and I were unable to resist unwrapping them and popping them in our mouths, though we always made a face afterward; they tasted like medicine. Unlike Harry and Esther, Morris paid his own rent. He did not come often to our apartment, though he faithfully attended dinner parties when invited. He didn't drink too much and paid gallant attention to any unattached young women there. He was always civil to Esther, made no attempt to see Harry. Summer and winter, he left the hotel each morning and walked to an office downtown where he looked over his substantial investments. Stocky, with a bristling white mustache, he wore a straw hat in summer, a Homburg in winter, and carried a cane always. On Saturdays, he took Peter and me to Riverside Drive, where we would watch the trains, until 1937 when the new West Side Highway put them underground.

He had come from Budapest as a boy of fourteen and worked as an interpreter for the Immigration Service. He had seen terrible things—families sent back across the ocean because of a quick, inaccurate diagnosis of a tubercular child, people tricked into handing over good money by officials who insisted it was counterfeit—all the things people on the next-to-bottom rung do to exploit those on the bottom rung. He left the Immigration Service to start a small hotel near the piers. He bought a larger hotel. He sold steamship tickets to immigrants through agents in Europe, met the boats, drove the new arrivals to his hotel. My Grandmother Elizabeth stayed up late making box lunches for them, and Morris drove them to the railroad terminal the following morning. He put them on trains headed for wherever he thought they should go: Swedes to Minnesota, Finns to Michigan, Welsh to the coal mines of Pennsylvania. He settled America.

Once, when I was grown, I spent an afternoon in the library, reading through old city directories published before phones or phone books were common. In them, I could follow Grandfather's American dream. He was first listed in 1895, the year Father was born. His occupation was noted as "agent." The following year, he was listed as proprietor of a boarding house at 19 Rector Street. The year after that, he gave the same address, not as a boarding house but as a hotel. I suspect it is the listing that changed, not the quality of the building. Two years later, he listed a different hotel on Clarkson Street. The years after that his residence is at the Clarkson Street hotel, but his business is now a new hotel at Abingdon Square. That is the hotel Father remembered. Morris and Elizabeth's only child, their Alfie, was eight years old when the Abingdon Hotel first appeared in the city directory. I have a postcard of an elegant building with an awning-covered restaurant in the front. I also found the menu for Father's bar mitzvah dinner, given at the Abingdon Hotel on December 27, 1908:

Fruit cocktail   Celery   Olives
Essence de Volaille, Elizabethian [sic]
Petite Bouchee des Dames
Appolinaris   Sauterne
Basse Rayee a la Jeanne d'Arc
Pommes de Terre, Duchesse
Cotelette de Poulet Nouveau Demoiselle Liberte
Petits Pois a l'Anglais
Burgundy
Sorbet Abingdon
Royal Squab au Cresson, Canape Diana
Pomona Salade
Pommery Brut
Amandes Tartes Glace Alfred
Petit Fours   Bonbons   Fruits   Fromage
Demi Tasse
Apricot Brandy   Cigars

That is the bar mitzvah dinner of a hotel kid!

Alfred must have pestered waiters and maids, hung around the kitchens, perhaps even played Elevator Free-

Fall—the postcard boasted of an elevator. He was the only other hotel kid Peter and I ever knew. It was a pity he did not talk much about the Abingdon. What stories we could have told each other!

A few years after Morris moved into the Taft, he married a woman he had met on a cruise, thirty years younger than he, with a son my age. Mother called her a professional widow. When she spoke of Grandfather's new wife, her voice, low to begin with (telephone operators generally answered her, "Yes, Mr. Lewis"), descended into the bass register. Grandfather Morris moved his old-fashioned furniture out of the Taft and into an apartment uptown, with his new family. Once a month, like a dutiful son, Father took us to dinner at his father's new apartment. After Morris died, the widow moved to California with her son and the family silver Morris had willed her. "That was your Grandmother Elizabeth's silver," Mother said. Pause. Then, in a register so low it was like glaciers humming, "That widow!"

Esther and Harry lived at the Taft the rest of their lives. When I was fourteen, I saw them on the mezzanine, seated together on a sofa, talking quietly. They asked me not to tell Mother; they said it would upset her. A bad cold the week of Harry's death prevented Mother from attending his funeral.

The hotel was a refuge for many people. Father's boss —a vice-president, a man who worked downtown (we said the word with awe)—had a brother who also worked at the Taft. One brother was the man our father had to ask for permission to do things; the other guarded the employee time clock, making sure everyone checked in and out.

For Father's boss and his brother, for Mother and Father, Harry and Esther, even for the strikers, who God knows had their share of grievances, for all but Morris, with a sunny new apartment and a new wife and child, hotel life was like a French fairy tale: inside, magic; outside, dark and wintry woods.

five

The earliest job I had, at the age of ten or so, was help-
ing Aunt Dolly and Uncle Al at the newsstand on Saturdays, neatening up the piles of the *New York Times,* the
Herald-Tribune, the *News,* the *Mirror,* the *Journal-Ameri-
can,* and the *Brooklyn Daily Eagle.* Once, I wrapped boxes
of Kotex in plain brown paper in the back room. (Mother
laughed when I told her what I had been doing that particular Saturday afternoon but wouldn't tell me what was
funny.) I was paid twenty-five cents an hour.

Peter worked at the jewelry stand across the lobby, next
to the Coffee Shop. Almost anyone who went into the
Coffee Shop, certainly anyone who waited on line outside
for a table, had time to examine the displays there: Mickey
Mouse watches, bronzed miniature Empire State Buildings, rings with tiny real stones, and earrings with large
fake ones. Peter's job was to polish the fingerprints off the
display cases. We were not as friendly with the couple

who owned the jewelry stand as we were with Dolly and Al. The woman was almost frighteningly good-looking; she had a superb body and wore skin-tight dresses. Her husband once promised Peter a cigarette lighter when he came to work that afternoon. It was all Peter and I could talk about as we sat perched on counter stools at the Coffee Shop before going to work that particular Saturday. I walked Peter back to the jewelry stand and waited with him as the man gave Peter a booklet of Taft matches and laughed. I could never stand him after that.

No one talked about role models at the time, but Mother saw that Peter and I needed more of a male presence than Father, making his rounds, his hands clasped behind his back, had time to be. Thinking to find a young man who would stay in the apartment on weeknights, help us with our homework, teach us to play ball, improve our posture, and bring us into mainstream America, she called Columbia University for a tutor. A young ball-playing student named Joe came for his interview wearing a college sweater with blue piping. He might have arrived out of an old black-and-white college campus musical instead of the subway. We immediately went out and bought blue-and-white felt football pennants inscribed "Columbia" to thumbtack on our bedroom wall alongside the banners from Cornell (the country's leading hotel school). But Joe's plans changed and he wasn't able to join us. He recommended a friend instead, Bob Lax.

Mother never fully registered the differences between Bob and Joe. Bob was a lanky poet, half waif, half wraith. His college roommate, Tom Merton, often came to visit him at the hotel and accompany us to the Roxy. In *The Seven Storey Mountain,* Merton's account of his spiritual quest and his life as a Trappist monk, he described Bob as a "kind of combination of Hamlet and Elias . . . a potential prophet but without rage"—a heady description for a stringbean college junior.

In our bedroom, Bob, legs jackknifed to his chin in an easy chair he had dragged in, drank milk by the quart and talked. Tom, on the floor, and Peter and I, on our beds, listened to Bob on books, spiritual rebirth, the small town where he was born. His descriptions of Olean, New York, were so vivid we walked its streets in our heads. Bob and Tom both tried to explain eternity to us. "What happens after eternity?" we asked. "More," said Tom. "What after more?" "A hundred times more than everything since time began," said Bob, adding, "And that's just the first minute." Peter looked as if he were going to cry; Merton looked a little upset himself.

The only walks we took with Bob were to the Roxy. We never played ball in the park. Bob tried to take me to a football game at Columbia, but he had never been to the stadium and we got lost on the subway. Still, Mother was very fond of him. She would come into our bedroom, stand near the door, and listen to him with a distant smile on her face. Though she rarely gave up control of a conversation, Bob was one of the few people she did not interrupt.

One Monday afternoon, Bob told us excitedly that he and Tom had found a brahmachari and were keeping him in their dormitory room. A brahmachari is a Buddhist monk. This particular brahmachari—probably the first ever hidden in a college dorm—had been sent by his order to attend the Chicago World's Fair of 1933. He arrived too late for the exposition and too broke to return home. Anyone dedicated to vows of poverty was a likely prospect, sooner or later, for Room Service. He visited us often, sitting cross-legged next to Peter on his bed. Peter, glancing nervously at him, moved down next to Tom on the carpet. The brahmachari might have been in his forties; it was hard to tell. His head was shaved, he wore a messy white sheet under his ragged overcoat and heavy wool socks under his sandals, and he was unintelligible, all of which distracted observers from specifics. He was immensely cheerful and irremediably optimistic about finding his way home. He turned out to be right, eventually finding a wealthy supporter who provided the money to send him back to India. I went with Bob to his farewell dinner but fell asleep before he spoke and missed his final unintelligible insights.

Mother eventually noticed that Bob wasn't anything like ball-throwing, ball-catching Joe, so Bob left too, returning to his dormitory room and leaving us as far from the mainstream as ever. Maybe farther. It was not that we never saw men. Among the regulars at Mother's lunches there were bachelors, not very hardworking, with enough time on their hands to kill an hour or so or the afternoon. Three in particular were frequent visitors. The two Jerrys, as we called them, were good-looking, had gone to Ivy League schools, and laughed easily. The third, Frankie the Fixer, was a fire inspector, an orphan who joined the Fire Department after high school for lack of other possibilities and who felt permanently angry and shortchanged. He covered his mouth when he laughed, as if he were ashamed of any good feelings. Once, he showed Peter and me a blackjack, surprisingly small, smaller than a salad fork, with which he gave us painful, instructional taps on the arm, chuckling.

The Jerrys would be called walkers a few years later, unattached men with unromantic attachments to women friends. Walkers generally took their women friends shopping, but Mother didn't shop—or even walk, if she didn't have to. Instead, the Jerrys filled in as extra men at dinner and cocktail parties. They brought her sterling silver bar tools and other thoughtful thank-you gifts; Frankie brought her free cosmetics and other merchandise he picked up from manufacturers on his route. He brought Peter and me illegal fireworks he confiscated. Mother took them away from us as soon as he left. "They'll put out your eye." She wouldn't say that in front of him, though, or tell him not to bring us any more. Frankie knew his way around City Hall and the Powerhouse, as Saint Patrick's Cathedral and the influential Catholic hierarchy were called. A Times Square hotel draws the vice squad like roadkill does crows, and Father never knew when he might need Frankie.

I don't think any of the three considered an affair with Mother, though Frankie would have been tempted, out of malice if nothing else. They would not have hung around so obviously if they had. Long-ago Venetians called men like this *cicisbei*—gallants who kept wives busy while their husbands worked, a relationship generally platonic, though of course there were always missteps and slip-ups.

Occasionally Father would get fed up. Even though we weren't old enough to recognize his irritation as jealousy, we were sometimes jealous, too. But we were so delighted with the Jerrys' attention that we would have overlooked almost anything. The Jerrys and Frankie were sufficiently kindhearted or shrewd to visit with Peter and me whenever they came to the apartment. They sat next to us when we were together in the Grill or Tap Room and whispered silly jokes to us. We thought of them as our favorite adults. We failed to notice that none of them spent time with us when Mother wasn't around. Though we never thought much about Uncle Al at the newsstand (who, with his checked jackets and high-polish fingernails, looked exactly like Nicely-Nicely in *Guys and Dolls*), it was he who took us to the only baseball game we ever saw, treated me to the fights at Madison Square Garden where I sat happily at the age of ten in a miasma of cigar smoke, and laid Peter's ten-cent bets on the ponies. "Looking good, pally," he'd say as I passed the newsstand on my way to school. "Looking like a million."

$\mathscr{L}$ate one afternoon, Mother overheard me asking Bridie for help with my homework. Curious, she sat down beside me, smelling of Blue Grass perfume and White Horse Scotch and looked over my shoulder at the page. "Look. Divide the nine into the five . . . the number below the line into the number above."

Wow!

She went back to her bedroom, pleased with herself. Awed, I followed her. "Gee, I didn't know you were an apartment-house mother."

"A what?"

Apartment-house mothers, I explained, cooked, cleaned house, and helped their children with their homework. (People who lived in single-family homes were so far outside my frame of reference that I didn't have a word for them.) Though some of our relatives had maids and even cooks, I sensed that the mothers were more involved in their families' lives, in their own lives even, than our mother was in hers or ours.

Some time after that, Mother and Father decided to rent a house in the suburbs for a year, just to try, they explained. They found a two-story Tudor bungalow, dark brown beams glued to white stucco walls, in New Rochelle, on a mixed block of Cape Cods and French Provincials. New Rochelle was the setting of a musical by George M. Cohan, *Forty-Five Minutes from Broadway*. A Broadway-smart prizefight promoter tries to make a new life for himself. And fails.

We would have a yard. Peter and I would get bikes. "Won't that be fun?" Although this was our chance to become the real American boys we had always wanted to be, Peter and I had misgivings. Would it be like camp in New Hampshire, where we were sent each July and August to stand on the far edges of a baseball field, waiting for a ball that never came and that we could not have caught if it had? What about free comic books? After school every afternoon we leafed through the rack of comic books at the newsstand, taking the new arrivals upstairs, returning them the next day. "Aunt Dolly will save them for you and send them up to New Rochelle, just like camp." Once or twice during the summer, Dolly would mail us a tight cylinder of twenty to thirty rolled-up comic books.

"What about the movies?"

"There's a movie in New Rochelle."

"A movie?" Just *one*? We went to the Roxy, the Capitol, the Strand, Loew's Ziegfeld, Loew's State, the Criterion, the Globe, the Victory, the Apollo, the New Amsterdam. *A* movie?

Still, one Sunday in spring we drove up the Hutchison River Parkway in a brand-new 1939 Dodge Father had bought for our suburban adventure. The parkway banked and curved through grassy borders and past sculpted bushes and trees. Exiting, we drove into a picture-perfect village. Broad, tree-shaded streets. Front yards. Old horse chestnut trees. Oaks. Acorns. Norman Rockwell might have lived in New Rochelle. In fact, he did.

When we pulled up to our house, we saw a kind of cottage, a dozen yards in from the street. A mini-sidewalk ran from the street to the front door past grass and trees. (I was to learn this was called, simply, "the walk." The wider sidewalk parallel to it that led to the garage was called "the driveway.") Fifteen floors closer to the street than we were used to, it all seemed very exposed. Even from the street, we could see furniture in the living room and, in the dining room, only slightly veiled by gauze curtains, a polished oval dining table. I noted nervously that anyone who wanted to could walk up and watch us eating.

Bridie came to help unpack and stayed with us while we settled in. The downstairs bedroom was Mother's, and Father's when he came. The largest of the small bedrooms upstairs had dormers. What could be more American than dormers! I even cracked my head on the slanted ceiling the first few mornings I awoke. Hadn't Mickey Rooney done that in an Andy Hardy movie? The second bedroom was for Bridie or Grandma Esther. There was a third bedroom, a tiny room down the hall that Peter or I could sleep in if we wanted to. Never having experienced the luxury of a bedroom to myself, except when I was sick, I tried it a few times, but I got lonely.

I missed street noise. After dark, it was a rare car that made its way down our street. Its headlights would march across the wall and up the ceiling. I lay in bed, smelling trees and grass through the open window, wondering why the headlights traveled upward across the ceiling when the cars drove in a straight line on the street outside. One night a large moth found its way into our bedroom. Peter and I convinced ourselves it was a bat; nothing could persuade us to sleep in that room for a week.

One of us slept downstairs with Mother, the other in the tiny bedroom down the hall.

Peter and I, exploring our new home, found a button hidden under the carpet beneath the dining room table. Experimenting, we found that when pushed, it buzzed in the kitchen. We couldn't wait to try it at dinner, delighted at the thought of sending Mother endlessly back and forth between the two rooms. We giggled as we heard the buzzer go off. Impressively, the first thing she did was look under the table. We never figured out how she knew.

When she told us we were going to the store to pick out our new bicycles, Mother must have seen the expressions on our faces. "Come on, you're big boys. You've ridden bikes."

In good weather, Bridie would take us to a bicycle rental store at the edge of Central Park. We'd walk our bikes across the street and ride them uncertainly around the park paths. Once, tough kids stopped us and demanded that we let them steal the bells on the handlebars. It didn't occur to us to refuse them or to bicycle away. Probably, surrounded by waiters, porters, and mail clerks whose only thought was to give us what we wanted, we hadn't learned how to react to people whose agendas didn't begin with making us happy. After that, we asked the rental store for bicycles without bells.

When we explained, Mother laughed. "New Rochelle's not like New York."

Mother didn't cook. After Bridie went back to the city, Grandmother came and made our breakfasts and dinners —the first Jewish cooking we had ever eaten. Out from the kitchen came potato pancakes, cottage cheese pancakes, buckwheat pancakes, Bisquick pancakes, all served with sour cream. Her recipes were sugary enough to pull the teeth out of our heads, her peas and carrots as sweet as other people's strawberry jam. She filled her strawberry pie, in fact, with a large jar of brilliant red A&P strawberry jam.

Carmen, slim, elegant, and chocolate colored, fixed our lunches and cleaned the house. Her husband, Ronald, an equally elegant gray-haired, lightly toasted man, chauffeur on a large Westchester estate, dropped her off in a gray Cadillac that his employer let him borrow. Carmen brought to work a cowed Dalmatian with whom we could play if we behaved ourselves. One afternoon, Mother was out with a friend and Peter and I were alone when Carmen began to chase us around the dining room table she had just polished. She was laughing and crying. She had a knife and at first we thought she wanted to kill us, then we realized she was threatening to kill herself. Peter ran into the kitchen to hide the rest of the knives. I was alone with a beautiful, unpredictable woman, the first of many times

I was to associate women and danger and find it exciting. (Actually, Mother was probably the first.)

"Don't do it, Carmen!" Peter pleaded. "What about Ronald?" A miscalculation. "Ronald! That son of a bitch devil!" "OK, OK," I said. "What about Rachel?" The Dalmatian. Carmen looked at me. "You think a *dog* gonna change my mind?"

Peter again: "What about Father Divine?" Carmen, puzzled, stopped running. I looked at Peter with disgust. "That was the other one!" He had confused Carmen with Amazing Grace, a cleaning lady who had been with us for only a few weeks before making her way back to Harlem and Father Divine. Distracted by Peter's question, Carmen put the knife down on the table, put on her coat and hat, and left. Peter and I made bologna sandwiches. By the time Mother came back from a late lunch, we had already washed our dishes. We said nothing about Carmen's wanting to kill herself or even leaving early; hotel kids don't squeal. We didn't say anything to Carmen, either, when she came to work the next day, and she never mentioned that afternoon to us.

When spoiled city kids move to the farm, the story goes, they learn that milk comes warm from a cow, not cold from a carton, that meat doesn't come prewrapped — that animals must be slaughtered to feed them — and that vegetables come from manure and hard work, not a paper bag. If Peter and I never reached that epiphany, at least we moved one level closer to the concept. We learned that food comes from a grocery store, not a waiter. Instead of the five-gallon cans of peas and peaches on Charlie the Steward's shelves, we ate from smaller cans of fruit and vegetables, just big enough for a meal. Instead of individual boxes of breakfast cereal that the waiters sliced open for us, we were introduced to giant boxes of corn flakes. (Confusingly, both the small cans and the large boxes were called family size.) When we saw black specks swimming in the milk on our cereal, we learned to check cereal boxes for ants. We checked our bread for mold before putting it in the toaster. We smelled the milk and cream before we poured them. We learned that what we left uneaten turned into garbage. Up until then, it had been whisked downstairs in the freight elevator. We learned that garbage smells. We took out the garbage.

If ever we were to become real American boys, this was it. Within two blocks of our house there was a country club whose greens made easy sledding in the winter, a well-preserved, white-painted wood cottage that once belonged to the author of "Home Sweet Home," a cemetery that we passed on the way to school (I whistled when I went past it, having read somewhere that that was what boys did, to keep their spirits up). We rode our bicycles down tree-shaded streets, stopping to fill our pockets with horse chestnuts. We cut them open, tasted their pulp, tried to make whistles out of them, set them on fire, threw them at targets, piled them on tables. We assumed that when school started and we came into contact with real American boys who had grown up there, they could let us in on what horse chestnuts were good for, but no one, not even the other kids who collected them, was ever able to do that.

In the fall, as we readied for school, buying new notebooks and pencils, we came home to hear Mother and Grandmother listening to the radio. Hitler had invaded Poland. They seemed very upset. We knew about Hitler, of course. Though we hadn't heard him, every kid made fun of his ranting, shouting unintelligibly with one arm raised in a salute, a pocket comb held under his nose for the mustache. Did she have relatives in Poland? we asked Grandmother. Maybe. Not close ones, she said. We dismissed Hitler.

From my sixth-grade-classroom window, I could see the New York World's Fair Trylon above the horizon, a huge triangular monolith. Next to it, though invisible from New Rochelle, sat an enormous globe called the Perisphere. Together, the futuristic duo was the icon of the fair, which was called "The World of Tomorrow." (Despite its name, the fair managed to completely ignore the Second World War, already underway.) Peter and I couldn't wait to see it. Every day we read of the exhibits and entertainments—model railroads, free Heinz dill pickle pins, television. Carmen and her husband, who had the use of his employer's Cadillac on his day off, took us one Saturday and returned us, tired and happy at the end of the day. After that, we complained whenever we had to ride in Father's new Dodge. Mother explained that though the Dodge was not as nice as the Cadillac, Father really owned the Dodge, while the chauffeur's car was merely borrowed. We didn't think that was much of a distinction. Father didn't own the Taft, he merely had the use of it, and we were all perfectly satisfied.

Peter and I didn't find as many friends at school as we had hoped. The children we met there had been together since the first grade. Our particular currency—free ice-cream sodas and sundaes—didn't work here. Once, three boys picked a fight with me in front of our house, pushing me, tripping me, punching me. Mother saw it and called out. To my astonishment, instead of stopping the fight, she told the boys they should choose just one of them to make it a fair fight. They did, and he beat me up easily. Now I had to take boxing lessons at the Y downtown. This should have made me even more of a real American boy, but I don't remember feeling that way. Although the first thing I learned—to hold my fists in front of my face—sounded like a good move, I found that giving yourself a bloody nose is no better than having someone else do it. I came home from school one day with my shirt hanging out of my trousers. Some boys, for no reason at all, had pulled it out on my way home. "What's a kike?" I asked.

Just before Christmas, on my way to school, I stopped at the edge of a group of boys surrounding a man in his car. Standing on tiptoe, I could see a catalogue in his hand, illustrating gifts that could be purchased with points. I shouted, "How do you get points?" Annoyed, the man looked up and said, "I'm after telling you all—by selling subscriptions to the *Saturday Evening Post.*" The youngsters who met his stringent criteria would be assigned an eight-block section of the neighborhood to canvas. A certain number of subscriptions sold—a number greater than the number of houses in the eight-block area—would get you a bicycle or a red wagon. My own goal was modest: a coin changer like the one conductors on the Fifth Avenue bus wore, which dropped pennies, nickels, dimes, and quarters into their hands. It cost fewer than a dozen points. I met the *Post*'s stringent criteria and received a sales territory close to my house.

Perhaps the suburbs hadn't yet made me a real American boy, even though I rode a bicycle down the same streets Norman Rockwell woke up to each morning. But selling subscriptions to the *Saturday Evening Post*—

founded by Benjamin Franklin—could be the ticket that would take me to that broad highway everyone else was marching down, strong, confident, and at ease. I picked up my free sample of the magazine and my order pad. Mother stood at the door and wished me luck, and I walked two blocks to my sales territory. I rang every doorbell along the first four blocks of my eight-block route. Only one man, at home with a cold and in his bathrobe, was there to answer the door. He explained that he already subscribed. Turning left, I walked down the block behind the streets I had just canvassed. There, too, only one man was at home. Though I didn't recognize him, he recognized me. "Hey, kid. I already told you. We subscribe." He explained that I was ringing the back-door bells to the houses I had just covered from the front.

In New Rochelle, only people with colds were home during the day. At the Taft, Mother and Bridie had always been home. In New Rochelle, Mother and Carmen were always home. Where was everybody? Though I argued with Mother that I had to make my sales calls after dinner, I soon learned that a classmate of mine had canvassed the same territory only two weeks before. Disillusioned with the magazine—Ben Franklin was just another con, like the three-card-monte tricksters on the street corner down from the Taft—I wouldn't let Mother subscribe, even though it would have been my only sale.

Worse was to come. Billy, who sat next to me in class, told me he had met Norman Rockwell, who had asked him to pose. Wow! A sort of friend of mine had become the realest American boy I or anyone else would ever know! "How's it going?" I'd ask, casually, on the mornings after he had been excused early from school to pose. "OK." "What do you do?" "Stand." How I envied him! That spring, the poster came out, for the March of Dimes campaign against polio. Billy looked like Billy, all right, except for the crutches! What a fake! Billy could run faster than I could! Even the fake blind man on Forty-ninth Street with the fake Seeing Eye dog that Peter used to pet didn't carry fake crutches! Another con—and a Norman Rockwell con, at that.

Someone stole Peter's bicycle. He left it leaning against a tree in our front yard. When he came out to run an errand for Mother, it was gone. "You should have put it in the garage," Mother told him.

I never knew why we moved to the suburbs. Maybe it was to get away from the four small rooms we'd been cooped up in for the past eight years. Maybe Mother and Father needed to get away from each other. Maybe Father had a girl. He managed to get to New Rochelle a few nights a week, sometimes in time for dinner, sometimes long after Peter and I had gone to bed. Someone had to be on call at the hotel twenty-four hours a day in case anything went wrong. Hadn't they thought of that before deciding to move to the country? He was on call two or three weeknights each week and at least one weekend a month.

What had Mother been thinking of? She couldn't drive. Although she said she'd learn, neither Peter nor I believed that a woman who had to look at her feet when she walked could learn to drive a car. She signed up for driving lessons but couldn't find an instructor who didn't make her nervous. She wasn't used to being told what to do. Friends from the afternoon canasta games or one of the Jerrys would drive up from the city to give her lessons. But the lessons quickly degenerated into chauffeuring expeditions. They'd go out to lunch, have a few drinks, do some shopping, and come back to the house without Mother's ever touching the wheel. Frankie the Fixer offered to take her to New York for her driving test. He promised she'd pass, "even if you run down every cop from Times Square to Central Park," but she was frightened of city streets. Without cold meat platters to entice friends from the city to visit, weeks passed between lessons. Not learning to drive, she was imprisoned even more securely in the suburbs than she had been at the Taft. It didn't occur to me for years that she might have wanted it that way.

Sometimes when Father came home late, Peter and I would wake to a shouting match downstairs. How would we feel if they divorced? Mother asked. We'd feel terrible. "Gee, Ma. Don't talk like that. You *can't* get divorced." Actually, the idea was pretty exciting, until she asked us who we'd want to live with. We thought about it. How could we live alone with Father? He was at work before we woke up and after we went to sleep. And despite—or because of—our year in the suburbs, we couldn't imagine being raised by Mother. Talking late at night in our dormered bedroom, we recognized that they had to stay together long enough for us to start life on our own. But when might that be—when I finished high school? When Peter did? How would we earn money? Now when we said they mustn't divorce, we really meant it. Then their fights subsided and their problem, whatever it was, disappeared from view.

On my eleventh birthday, Father drove up from the city with a special surprise—an ice-cream cake packed in an insulated box along with cartons of chocolate and strawberry sauce. The kitchen had surrounded the cake with dry ice to be sure it did not melt. We waited while Father dipped a cake knife into boiling water. He swore as he tried to chisel through the ice cream. "Goddamn it, Evelyn. This is like a rock." We boiled more water but finally had to settle for dishes of sauce. The cake wasn't soft enough to cut until we woke the next morning to find it a viscous puddle of white, brown, and pink. Each of us knew, without saying anything, that we were going back to the Taft.

$\mathcal{M}$other tried to make up for the failure of New Rochelle with a dog. Peter loved dogs: the little sausage that walked through the lobby with the tiny lady with the big hat, an old Irish terrier with a nappy brindle saddle that visited us whenever Mother's friend Annette came to play cards, Al and Dolly's fat terrier who stayed in their doggy-smelling suite all day and slept so much he might as well have been a variant, nocturnal species.

We went each year to the dog show at Madison Square Garden to wander through the aisles of cages in the basement, discussing which were our favorite breeds. Putting our hands into the cages to pet the dogs was risky. Either the dogs or their owners snapped at us. I gave any dog that looked the least bit surly a quick pat on the flank, my hands in and out of the cage like a flash. Peter petted more dogs than I, his hand closer to their jaws.

After we moved back into the Taft, Frankie the Fixer found us a Boston bull terrier that we named Trouble. He had a chocolate-brown face and a black shiny nose. He was a smart, affectionate little dog who sneezed a lot, as Boston terriers do. We'd race him in the halls. He was faster than we were but no smarter than our friends, whom we could always fool. Every sharp turn and idiosyncratic bypass in the mazy corridors was burned into our brains. We could feint Trouble out, dodging unexpectedly. He'd skid past us, his feet desperately scrabbling on the carpet to turn a sharp corner. When Trouble occasionally escaped into the hall, we would search the corridors calling his name. When we couldn't find him, Peter would cry. Mother would call Father and Father would call the security officers. More in the habit of inquiring about women than terriers in the rooms, they nevertheless knocked on each of the ninety-five guest rooms on our floor to ask if anyone had seen a small brown dog. They always found him, padding around the corridors.

Peter and I swore we'd walk Trouble before school and after dinner, but when it was cold or rainy or we were sleepy, we'd call a last boy and give him a quarter to walk Trouble for us. (A last boy is the last bellman on line, used by senior staff for tipless errands.)

Like the rest of us, Trouble was fed by Room Service. Each day, a waiter brought up, with the menus, a bowl of scraps collected by one of the kitchen workers. If the scraps were fattier than Mother thought good for Trouble, she'd call Room Service and ask them to boil some ground meat for him. I suspect, from the tempting smells that arose from his dish, that the kitchen probably poached the meat in beef broth.

During the war, foods were rationed; restaurants could serve only fish, chicken, and omelets on Meatless Tuesdays. One Meatless Tuesday, a union shop steward on the freight elevator noticed that a waiter was carrying a bowl of what seemed to be boiled hamburger on a tray.

"Who's the meat for?"

"The manager's dog."

Trouble.

six

*O*ur first month back from New Rochelle, Peter and I visited the Coffee Shop twice a day. The Roxy box office, just
a few yards away, helped make the restaurant popular. It
was a wonderful place to go for lunch before the show, or
for a soda afterward. The chorus boys and girls from the
Roxy would often sit at the counter in full makeup, grabbing a bite between shows. We were awed by them, too
shy to say hello when they smiled at us. One of the petti-
est of the girls came in every afternoon with a man in
his late fifties. Even when we were very young, we didn't
think he was her father.

During the Depression, when lunch was thirty-five
cents for a first course, main course, dessert, and coffee,
people sometimes asked the waitresses if they could have
their dessert and coffee when they came back after the
movie.

At other coffee shops, hungry customers hovered behind people at the counter and breathed on their necks

until they gobbled the last mouthful and got out of there, but at the Taft, we all waited in a line in the lobby, outside the glass door. The Coffee Shop manager would come out. "A seat at the counter. Anyone for a seat at the counter?" She'd smile at us. "Do you still want to wait for two? It won't be long." We always sat together, or at least separated by no more than one stool.

I liked to lean over the counter to watch Bill the Counterman make sodas. A glass eight inches high sat in an openwork metal holder that added another inch to its height. Bill smeared whipped cream around the sides of the glass, placed it under a syrup spout, pushed an inch of Crayola-colored syrup into it, and poured an inch of milk on top. He placed the glass under a spigot and pushed the handle away from him. Milk and syrup erupted together as soda water jetted into the glass. He dipped a scoop of ice cream from one of a dozen five-gallon containers in his work space and released it on top of the fizzy milk and syrup. Then he turned the spigot, this time toward him, releasing a gentle stream of soda that filled the glass. He floated a mound of whipped cream on top, picked up a maraschino cherry with his fingers, and nestled it on top. Sliding the glass across the marble counter, he filled out a check. Fifteen cents.

One time, I read a sign pasted on the window of the Coffee Shop: "Double Rich Dark Dutch Creamery Hot

Chocolate." It was bitterly cold on Seventh Avenue, and I could practically feel the boiling hot chocolate scorching my throat. I rushed in and grabbed a seat at the counter. "I'll have the double rich dark Dutch creamery hot chocolate," I said to Bill. He leaned over to break it to me gently. "Steve, that's just the regular hot cocoa."

Bill had blond hair slicked straight back and he was fat, with fingers like sausages. He wisecracked with us and with customers. Once, a man watching him make a soda asked Bill if the red syrup he was pouring into the glass was strawberry or raspberry. "If you can tell the difference," Bill said, "it's my treat." We used to tell Father what Bill had said, but instead of laughing with us, he swore, and we realized that repeating Bill's bon mots to Father would only get him fired. We each left a nickel tip at breakfast, ten cents at lunch, and fifteen cents at dinner on those special evenings when, as a treat, we were allowed to eat downstairs alone. Since candy and comic books within the hotel were free, our allowance was really our tip money.

We brought friends from the Lincoln School, a private, progressive school uptown we now attended, for sodas and sundaes, frosteds and floats. Our schoolmates were well-to-do Jewish kids who lived not in cold-water flats but in twelve-room apartments on Park Avenue or Central Park West. Their fathers (or mothers) owned department stores or were surgeons or judges. But when we brought our lunch to school, our classmates quickly and silently gathered around us in the cafeteria. Inside the brown paper bags, giant sandwiches from Room Service held prime rib dinners, cold, trimmed of fat, and minus the vegetables and watercress that would otherwise have garnished the plate, or ham and swiss on rye, two and a half inches high, wrapped in wax paper with a dill pickle slice neatly tucked inside the fold, or both. When we saw the looks on our classmates' faces, we knew, if we wanted them, they were ours.

Going through the class methodically, we had soon invited all the boys to the Roxy. (By then, Father received passes to the theater, and Peter and I went every week, even when the same movie ran for a month.) Afterward we took the boys back to the Taft and perched at the Coffee Shop counter. If power corrupts, hot fudge corrupts absolutely. Kids whose fathers could have bought the counter and transported it to their Park Avenue apartments were shackled to us even more firmly than Charley Ellis and our other friends on the relief. A boy whose father's name was on half the construction sites in Manhattan showed up every Saturday, just before lunch, for months.

Even as I invited my classmates to the Taft, I secretly awarded them demerits for accepting my invitations. Though I was now popular in the school halls, I still felt an outsider. I was suffering the age-old dilemma of royalty, rock stars, and Rockefellers—never sure that my friends were not in it only for what they could get, but unwilling to cut off the hot fudge and perhaps learn the truth.

*D*uring the summer, I helped out in Father's office. He thought the discipline would do me good, and I was delighted to get a paycheck—actually, an envelope with a few bills and some coins. I cared not so much for the money as for the equality. I had always been uncomfortable with the power behind my half of the friendship with bellmen, porters, waiters. I knew I was the boss's spoiled kid. Now we were lined up together at the payroll window, picking up our sealed brown envelopes.

At first, I opened envelopes and delivered mail and memos. When Father was irritated, everyone could hear him shout "Balls!" from behind his clouded glass wall. The clerks would giggle, glance at the boss's son out of the corners of their eyes, and go back to their typing. On my delivery route, I said hi to everyone I passed, much as I did when I hung around the lobby after school with nothing better to do. Not much discipline there—it was too much like what I did when I wasn't working.

Father moved me to bookkeeping, at the other end of the mezzanine, where the chief accountant patiently taught me about ledgers. Part of my job—the part I liked the most since it let me out of the office and I could stop and talk to my friends—was collecting the coins from the pay toilets in the men's and ladies' rooms on the mezzanine and in the lobby. In those days, before people came to their senses and insisted to the city that toilets be made free, only one stall was unlocked, for emergencies; all the others cost a nickel, later a dime. I unlocked the cash box attached to each door and took the nickels in a big canvas bag up to the bookkeeping office. There, I put them in a wonderful machine that counted them and spit them out in tight cylinders of twenty, waiting to be clumsily wrapped by me. After a few weeks of collecting and counting a few hundred dollars every other day from just two men's rooms and two ladies' rooms, I told Father he should tear out the guest rooms and replace them with toilets. I remember him looking at me, trying to decide if I was joking, probably praying that I was. I think I was an enigma to him. Once, out of patience, he turned to Mother and said, "He's been like that ever since I've known him."

A hotel has night auditors who start work before midnight and work until six in the morning, or later if they can't balance the previous day's receipts. Sometimes I would find them still there when I arrived at nine. I didn't know why someone would want to be a night auditor—

perhaps they hoped eventually to be promoted to a day job. My own position opened up after I misplaced the records of the hotel's receipts for one whole day: the guest rooms, the Grill Room, the Tap Room, the Village Room, the Coffee Shop, even the records of the postage stamps that were sold at the mail desk, everything except the nickels from the pay toilets, which I had sorted, wrapped, and safely locked away in the head bookkeeper's desk drawer. Someone, maybe I, found the receipts the next day, misfiled or under a pile of papers or possibly even upstairs in my room; meanwhile, the auditors had the night off, with pay.

I was sent to Miss Hirsch in personnel, next door to bookkeeping, and she transferred me to guest history, a small, hot room under the roof that held a file card for every visit of everyone who had ever stayed at the hotel: the room number, how long the guest stayed, and any changes he or she had requested, one card for each visit. A blue mark at the bottom of the card signified a credit problem. Anyone who sent us a letter of complaint had his card marked in red. Before sending the guest a three-day and then a six-month thank-you letter, the office checked guest history. Blue and red marks didn't get thank-yous. I filed cards all day. My cuticles bled. It took me a while to connect my loss of the hotel's receipts with my assignment to guest history.

One summer, I worked at the Taft's sister hotel, the St. George in Brooklyn Heights. I found taking the subway to Brooklyn an adventure, an indication of how sheltered I really was. The St. George was famous for its indoor swimming pool. It was a saltwater pool that Father said came from a saltwater stream under the hotel. I know they didn't pipe water in from the East River a block away; everyone would have died from infections not seen since the Dark Ages if they had. At one end of the pool, a waterfall splashed twenty feet down on those of us sturdy enough to stand under it, shoulders hunched, like prisoners taking a beating. When I got up early enough, I would have time for a swim and a beating before work. At lunchtime, I'd take my brown paper bag of thick roast beef sandwiches from the Taft and sit on a bench overlooking the river and lower Manhattan and smell the salt air.

When he was old enough, Peter worked one summer in a bank. "What's it like?" I asked. "Every time I look at the clock," he said, "and I must look at that clock a hundred times a day, it's always quarter to three."

The very best thing about living on Times Square was the Second World War, which came on the cusp of my adolescence. Aunt Mick, volunteering at the Pepsi-Cola booth in Times Square, wasn't as happy about the war as Peter and I. (Neither were millions of other men and

148

women with children old enough for war.) Our cousin, Mick's seventeen-year-old son, had enlisted in the Navy, training to be a dive bomber pilot. She cried nearly all the time. But for Peter and me, the war turned our neighborhood into a perpetual carnival, noisy, lively, and best of all, communal. We jostled and were jostled by crowds of young men just a few years older than we. They paid no attention to us, were not even aware we were there, but still we felt a part of it all.

We bought victory stamps for twenty-five cents, fifty cents, and a dollar, pasting them in special albums until we had enough to turn in for a war bond. Everyone sold them. The band singer in the Grill sold them to customers between sets. The cashier in the school cafeteria kept a roll next to the cash register. The flower shop folded them into corsages and sold them. Relatives gave us stamps on birthdays and Christmas. When we had nearly filled an album—which meant that we had pasted about sixteen dollars' worth into the booklet—we would wheedle Mother or Father out of the extra stamps we needed to turn the booklet in for a bond. "It's for the war," we whined. Like so many other profiteers, the war made us rich.

The war made everyone ravenous. We crowded the hot dog stands that lined the streets and devoured porky hot dogs, Kosher hot dogs, skinless hot dogs, hot dogs that popped when you bit into them and splashed greasy juice in your face, hot dogs baked in corn batter. We washed them down with watery orange drink, watery lemonade, and watery piña colada, a frothy mixture of artificial pineapple and artificial coconut. In wartime, everybody ate, literally, as if there were no tomorrow.

Ernie the Porter returned to the hotel on leave from boot camp. He must have had nowhere else to go. He was the youngest porter, a few years older than I, with a red nose and acne. Peter and I took him to lunch and to the Roxy, perhaps to *A Yank in the RAF*. It had run there for so long we could say the lines with Tyrone Power. Afterward, we drank ice-cream sodas at the Coffee Shop counter. Ernie's nose grew redder and his eyes filled. "I'll never forget you guys," he told us. "Just think. The manager's kids." Our own eyes filled, too. We were doing our part, just like Tyrone Power in the RAF. Ernie thanked us again before setting off for the Greyhound station that would take him back to camp. We walked him as far as the penny arcade on Eighth Avenue. At the penny arcade, we joined swarms of other kids not yet old enough to wear a uniform. We punched nickels into machines that let us shoot down Japanese fighter planes and torpedo Nazi ships. We went downstairs to the shooting range in the basement, where, for a quarter, we could shoot real rifles that snuffed candles, slapped down promenading ducks, hit brass gongs, and knocked over chipped painted faces with caricatured Japanese features. There were no pinball machines—Mayor LaGuardia detested them and they were illegal in New York, but he let us shoot at anything that moved. It would be a long while before Ernie could shoot as well as we.

We were combat ready. At school, instead of swimming meets, we learned how to abandon ship, leaping from the pool's edge into what we were told would be burning oil. In science class, we learned to identify aircraft whose silhouettes were flashed on a screen in the darkened physics lab. Unless we were attacked by one of our own planes, though, I was out of luck—the only outline I recognized was a double-fuselage Lockheed.

Our school was among the most progressive in the city, the faculty equally divided between Trotskyites and Stalinists, though I had no idea what those things were. I knew about Stalin, of course. The Russians were our allies. We sang "Meadowlands," the Red Army song, in music class, in Russian. We sang Chinese songs, too. "Farewell, darling, I must go. Let me not be late. With my comrades meet the foe at the Northern Gate."

Nothing at P.S. 69 or in New Rochelle had prepared us for the bright and moneyed prodigies around us. A girl asked if I intended to run the hotel when I was grown. "I don't think so," I told her. "My father doesn't own the hotel, he's the manager." "Oh, I'm so sorry," she apologized, her soft ninth-grade cheek growing red.

My friends were not the children of the rich but part of a small circle of European refugees, the children of diplomats, displaced intellectuals, and other exiles. Gus was a Yugoslav, and from him I learned of the deep divisions between the different partisan groups. Michael was German but, having escaped early to Britain, spoke with an elegant British accent. Diego, whose father had been the Spanish Loyalist defense minister, had escaped, barely, during the civil war. Grandma Esther was very fond of him but couldn't pronounce "Diego." She settled for "Dago," and when he greeted her in the apartment, so did he.

I learned to say "bourgeois" and grew sullen. Mother said, "You used to be such a happy little boy," which turned me more sullen. My friends' mothers, uprooted from Hamburg, Sarajevo, or Prague, made new friends, organized summer vacations in other people's guest houses, reconfigured their lives to make do without cooks or maids. Their fathers sat at home dispiritedly. They smiled wanly at me and their children's other American friends and waited until they could return to Europe and take up their professions again. Their children hovered between another place and time and an uncertain future. Our mutual rootlessness drew us close.

The high energy of wartime and the near-total exclusion of traditional academic subjects should have sent our adrenaline through the roof; in fact, we were just as bored as those prewar students who had been forced to study algebra and momentum. Whenever we could, we cut school to go to the movies. On Forty-second Street, the Laff Movie showed old two-reel comedies—Leon Errol, Chaz Chase, El Brendel, Laurel and Hardy—continuously. For as long as we sat through the show, we never saw a repeat of the picture we had walked in on. At least, I don't think we did; the films were so similar it is hard to be sure. I sat in the warmth of the smelly theater, surrounded by laughing soldiers and sailors, connected to them all by Laurel and Hardy. I'd stay until I'd miss hors d'oeuvres if I didn't get home. Then I'd make my way through Times Square among crowds of soldiers and sailors so excited by the limitless possibilities of the city and so dazzled by choice that all they could do was walk aimlessly up and down.

The neon-lit signs in Times Square had been extinguished for the duration. A new Camels billboard sent huge smoke rings of Con Edison steam floating out of the mouth of a giant painted, smiling sailor. (No one knew then that smoking was riskier than air raids.) The city was darkened not to hide Manhattan from Nazi planes but to eliminate the glow the nighttime city created miles out to sea. It could outline freighters and troop ships and make it easy for enemy submarines to target them. Blackouts were my favorite part of the war. I was a deputy air warden, assisting the air warden. The air warden was Father. We wore steel helmets and patrolled the streets in front of the hotel at night, watching for glimmers of light from behind the blackout drapes that covered each window. When he spotted a light, we counted the windows up and over to discover which room it was; then I went inside and told the hotel security officer, who called the guest and, if no one answered, went up with a passkey and turned off the light. We patrolled Seventh Avenue and Fifty-first Street for as long as it took to eliminate every crack of light. The longer we stayed out in our matching steel helmets, the better I liked it. Peter wasn't invited to help save New York. Far from defending my true friend and companion, I took advantage of his absence to stick it to him, explaining to Father that, at twelve, he was too young to be out.

More importantly, my growing interest in sex also left Peter behind. In the lobby, I became aware of unattached women. A drunken girl staggered through the Coffee Shop, lipstick smeared on her mouth, and above it and below it, too. My heart beat faster. I finished my ice cream and followed her into the lobby to see what she was going to do. What she did was pass out. By the time I had signed the check, she was on the floor a few feet from the Coffee Shop door, being helped to her feet by the assistant manager. I walked by, not daring to look, as she apologized incoherently.

I watched soldiers and sailors pick up girls in short skirts, upswept hair, and thick makeup, provocatively imitating Ida Lupino's imitation of a bad girl. On Broadway, I was fascinated by glossy eight-by-ten stills in front of the girlie shows and at the bottom of the stairs that led to the taxi dance halls on the second floor. Eyebrows plucked, wet lips parted, hands folded gracefully on top of cleavage or cupping breasts, they were an open invitation to every man who passed. I found out, though, that the invitation could be quickly rescinded when I tried to buy a ticket to the Tango Dance Palace or the Honeymoon Lane.

Losing interest in anything that did not involve the possibility of thighs, breasts, or tongues, for the first time I had little to say to Peter. If he wanted to hang around me and my friends, I told him to beat it. "You're just a little kid." I was hurtful, though never as hurtful as I might have been. We'd been too close for me not to hold some things back. I never said to him, for example, that he was short. I knew how disappointed he was that he would never be six feet. Although he brought it up often, wanting desperately to be tall, I knew that the subject was not one I could ever raise.

I grew street-smart. I knew the street vendors who offered dancing paper clowns (nowadays, they are made of plastic) a foot and a half tall, miraculously hopping up and down on the sidewalk without visible means of support. I could spot the confederate at the edge of the crowd, hands clasped behind his back, who alternately pulled and loosened the invisible thread that made the clown jiggle and dance.

Walking home once, I spotted a man coming toward me nod to another man leaning against a lamppost, reading a newspaper. The newspaper reader peeled off and started following another man, just walking past. I turned and followed the follower, curious to see if I could shadow a private eye. After a block I got bored and turned around again and went home.

Another time in the lobby, a man sidled up to me. "Can't say where this come from," he whispered, looking down meaningfully at a diamond ring in his cupped hand. "If I didn't need the cash, I could sell it for five times as much, but you can have it for a hundred bucks." I marveled that he could be dumb enough not to spot that I was just thirteen or, worse, to think a thirteen-year-old was a prospect for a stolen ring, or especially to think I wouldn't know it was glass, not stolen. I no longer remember how I knew all this—any more than you remember when you learned how to catch a ball.

Everybody assumes that growing up in a Times Square hotel was a crash course in sex. Before we came to the Taft, when it was still the Hotel Manger, it had an unsavory reputation, even for Times Square. Just mentioning the Taft was good for a laugh in the burlesque houses down the street, but Father eventually transformed the hotel so that high-school students could stay there on spring break without the school board firing the principal. "Even ministers stay here now," Mother said. When I was older, she told me that one security officer—that is, a house dick—stayed on after Father became manager. She asked him, "What in the world did you do here in the old days?" "You know," he replied, embarrassed. "Sometimes people stayed too long in the rooms."

But while suburban kids our age were staggering home drunk at two in the morning or sneaking girls into their house when their parents left town, we were waving goodnight to a house dick. In a lobby that surged with sexual possibility, we ran a merciless, loving gauntlet of proxy aunts and uncles: porters, bellmen, elevator operators.

If I had had more sense or nerve, I would have asked a house dick to fix me up. The house dicks were probably scared of me, the son of the boss, these guys who had enforced a hierarchy of authority their whole working lives, but I didn't know that. Bulky men in blue serge suits, they stood around the lobby, planted like rocks. I think they were called flatfoots not because of fallen arches but because of the way they stood, their center of gravity around their ankles. They were mostly retired vice-squad cops, hired because they knew every hooker who worked Seventh Avenue. House dicks also watched out for peelers, walkaways, key picks, weepers. Using counterfeit claim checks, peelers could walk up to the coatroom and get a coat for a quarter. Leave your suitcase unguarded and a walkaway picked it up—if caught, it was "sorry, my mistake"—checked it across the lobby at the porters' desk, then picked it up the next day. Key picks took your key after you had slid it toward the front desk clerk, and went through your room. Weepers—I forget what they were, but they were bad news. House dicks could even spot guests who just looked funny. They had a nose for funny, having spent their entire working lives looking for it and cleaning up after it. A guest would try to leave the hotel without paying, sometimes even from off the roof.

If a guest dies in a room, and there is a "Do Not Disturb" sign on the door, how many days will a chambermaid walk past it before telling the floor housekeeper? Who will the floor housekeeper call? Well, she might call the assistant manager, but who do you think he'll call? A house dick. After midnight, the assistant managers, dignified men in striped pants, went off duty. Their place was taken by house dicks. Who are you going to want at three in the morning? Not somebody in striped pants.

The tabloids used to write about two-fisted Johnny Broderick, a detective famous for beating up thugs sufficiently slow-witted to pull a gun on him. He sent them first to the hospital and then to the pen. Outside the pages of the *Daily Mirror,* he'd have been called a sadist. Father gave him a free room. I think it was listed as the headquarters of the Johnny Broderick Benevolent Association. He must have been the only member. Say someone drops dead, six feet from the door to the Tap Room or the elevators. The corpse can't be moved until a coroner or an assistant coroner comes to inspect it. It can be covered over with a blanket, that's all. Now suppose the coroner and assistant coroner are busy, away for the weekend, or just don't like the Taft. Maybe the Waldorf-Astoria didn't need a tough cop on their side (I bet they did), but a Times Square hotel certainly did.

Once they closed the Tap Room. A sign was posted on the glass doors saying that it had been raided. Father explained that a plainclothesman with a companion had ordered drinks at the bar the week before. After being served, the detective told the bartender that he had just served a homosexual. It was then illegal to run a gathering place for homosexuals. (So was refusing to serve someone who was not gay. Bartenders not only had to know how to mix a Singapore sling, they needed sexual radar.) The raid was a setup. Father didn't know why. He spoke to Frankie and the case was dismissed, probably on grounds as spurious as the original charge.

Toward the end of the war, I was sixteen. My friends and I were picking up girls ourselves, draggled bouquets not yet plucked by boys in uniform a few years older than we. I took one, prettier than most, out in a rowboat. We kissed. She told me she was from Provo, Utah, and was married to a sailor. She was nineteen. She gave me her phone number and I called her a few times, but she wouldn't see me, either because she was relieved that we hadn't made love that night or because she was disappointed. Sometimes I think it was one, sometimes, the other.

The night of August 15, 1945, when victory was announced—VJ Day—Peter and I walked through the pandemonium of Times Square. I've read that two million people were there. I roamed for hours, trying to fix the scene in my mind so that I would remember it always. Looking back on it now, I realize I can no longer distinguish between what I really saw and what came out the next week in *Life*.

seven

The Taft was becoming what was probably the most profitable hotel in New York City. Money was part of Alfred and Evelyn's life for the first time since they left the Knickerbocker. They went to elegant restaurants like Voisin and the Marguery and to corny nightclubs like Leon and Eddie's. They'd leave the apartment in a rush—always late—smelling of Scotch, cigarettes, and perfume. Sometimes they took us with them to steak houses and Italian restaurants that had once been speakeasies. Mother wore chic black, had her hats made by Mr. John, left restaurants always wobbly, holding onto my arm or Peter's or Father's. Once out, she wanted to stay out. "Let's go someplace else. Let's not go home yet." None of us appreciated how much she depended on momentum to carry her on once she left the hotel.

She took Dolly to lunch at "21." Since "21" was also a major wholesale liquor distributor and the Taft was a major customer, Mother was treated imperially—her favorite style. She and Dolly would come home a little tight, carrying paper napkins in their purses wrapped around "21"'s tiny checkerboard squares—chunky rectangles of alternating marzipan and chocolate cake, rimmed with raspberry jam and chocolate icing. When Father told her that Paul in the pastry kitchen could easily make them up for her, she made a face and said that that would be no fun.

Father took me to Luchow's for the giant apple pancake with *preiselbeeren* he remembered from his own youth. (Until I went there, I thought it was a Chinese restaurant, Loo Chow.) Mother took me to lunch at Chambord, under the Third Avenue El, where Roger Chauveron created a paradise of food for deep-pocketed New Yorkers. *Pommes de terre soufflées* came with practically everything: hot air bubbles surrounded by the thinnest surface of potato. They had to be eaten whole, of course. If you put your fork in one, it would instantly deflate, causing the people at the next banquette, who had learned white wine with chicken, red with meat, the month before, to glance at you out of the corner of their eyes. I had learned not to puncture my *soufflées* at home.

Instead of books for my birthdays, I now asked for French dinners. At the Colony, owner Gene Cavallero, a friend of Mother and Father's, treated me to a 1934 Comte de Vogüe Musigny, setting a standard for red wine I have not since been able to afford. At an expensive country inn, I returned a bottle of Aloxe-Corton. I thought it was too tannic, too sour, corky, who knows what I thought? Mother looked at me with shining eyes, her firstborn returning his first unsatisfactory order, a chip off her own block.

They went to Europe, bringing back embroidered handkerchiefs with hand-rolled edges and monograms for Peter and me. Handkerchiefs were Mother's gift of choice, I suppose because they didn't weigh much and took up almost no room in a suitcase. Every old lady in Valduz must have stayed up late rolling those edges each summer.

As Europe opened up and stranded European employees were able to return home, promotions became available. Monsieur Martin's sous-chef was promoted, a mixed privilege that brought with it increased salary and prestige but also a litany from Mother—"ice-cold," "swimming in butter"—followed by the slam of a phone. The sous-chef's brother was maitre d' of the first-class dining room on the French Line's flagship, the *Liberté*. Would we like him to arrange a small dinner for us, just the family, some night when the ship was in port? It would be his brother's special pleasure to have the chef fix us a little something in one of the private dining rooms in first class while the ship was restocking. We met the chef in his office, which was much nicer than Father's, we noted, and he took us through the first-class kitchens, which were much nicer and larger than ours. (The previous flagship, the *Normandie,* destroyed during the war, had a kitchen staff of two hundred.) I was awestruck as I watched a kitchen helper, not much older than I, braise some endives in flaming brandy. "Who's that for?" I asked the chef, since the ship was supposed to be passengerless. The chef glanced over at the boy. "His dinner."

In those days, Mother was suffused with longing to do nice things for me. I mentioned one day that my hair looked thin. She found a salon on Madison Avenue where they rubbed pepper compound into my scalp and sent me home with other jars so that I could give myself dandruff treatments before going to bed. I was doing poorly in school—not surprising, given Times Square and the Laff Movie and my feeling generally poleaxed by adolescence. She sent me to a psychiatrist on Park Avenue one afternoon a week. She signed me up for dancing lessons at Arthur Murray. She wanted to do more.

With two years of high school left, it was time to begin thinking about college. Mother put on a black dress and a Mr. John hat, and Smitty the cab driver drove her uptown to my progressive school. She flashed a smile at the principal that shone right through her veil and the cloud of cigarette smoke that hovered in front of it. She wanted to talk about college; he wanted to talk about my leaving his school. Perhaps, he suggested, I would do better out of the city at a preparatory school, one with more discipline and a more conservative curriculum than Lincoln's, in an environment with fewer distractions. In other words, no Times Square.

"A prep school!" Back in Smitty's taxi, with me at her side, she was exultant. I'd learn to play ball and stand straight and apply myself. Then we'd apply to Harvard. Why not? With the Taft's occupancy rate at over 90 percent, the best in the city, Harvard seemed a natural expectation. We had relatives in Boston. "You like your cousin Barbara. Harvard's the perfect place for you. You just have to apply yourself." She nodded happily as if that was settled, another hurdle overcome.

That spring, we used Father's gas ration coupons to visit red-brick prep schools with white steeples looking over the tobacco valleys of Connecticut. Admissions officers in tweed jackets and penny loafers, looking like well-preserved grasshoppers, bent before the force of Mother's vivid presence. Yes, they could see that I wasn't being fully challenged. Yes, they were sure I was a lovely boy. A hotel. How interesting. How unusual. After we left, out came the handkerchief from the tweed breast pocket, a mop of the brow, and "Jesus God!"

I had no opinion about my future myself or even a sense that where I went to school was any of my business. The war produced the least rebellious generation of American youth. Boys a year or two older than I were sometimes shot for disagreeing with authority. I followed Mother and Father helplessly into one Founder's Hall after another, all smelling of wax and furniture polish, until I received a letter welcoming me to the community of lovely young boys at the Loomis School in Connecticut. Mother invited the admissions officer to come stay at the Taft if he and his wife found themselves in New York. Peter looked betrayed. Never mind; he would be joining me the next year. Frankie the Fixer found a family with young children, just outside Philadelphia, with a real house and a real yard, for Trouble.

When Peter and I returned home on vacation or school break from our Connecticut prep school, we called our parents' men friends "Sir." We called Uncle Corny "Sir." In fact, we called just about everybody except the waiters and the bellmen "Sir." For Mother, that alone made Loomis worth the tuition.

Sometime during the year when Peter and I were off at school, Mother turned our bedroom into a dining room and our bathroom into a tiny kitchen with a real refrigerator, a toaster-broiler, and a couple of hot plates. She wasn't evicting us; the hotel carpenters opened up our suite to the next room down the hall.

For the dining room, she took an old hotel couch, had the back sawed off, and recovered it with red leather, so that it looked like one of the Tap Room banquettes. Waiters still brought up room service tables, and whoever was not seated at the banquette pulled up a hotel chair. She had a TV set—so new then there was just Milton Berle and wrestling—built into the wall, so that whoever sat at the banquette could watch Gorgeous George smash some other longhaired muscle man onto the canvas while we ate.

With a new kitchenette in place, it was natural that she would think of fixing us a homecooked meal when we returned from school. She had spoken of cooking for us in the past, generally once in the spring and once in the fall. When the days warmed in April or May and again when they cooled in October, the breezes that blew into our fifteenth-floor windows seemed to hold the promise of something closer to life's meaning, if only she would do her part.

It took five weeks, more or less, from the day she decided to cook until we ate. Though she offered to cook whatever Peter and I wanted, we knew that anyone who cooked once every six months might find some things too challenging. We always asked for California hamburgers. Now every fast-food chain puts lettuce and tomato and some kind of mayonnaisey dressing on hamburgers, but years ago, on restaurant menus at least, that was called a California hamburger.

"What do you want with your hamburgers?" Mother asked.

"Creamed spinach."

"You boys have that all the time. I might as well have Chef fix everything." There was nothing like a California hamburger, still sizzling from the toaster-broiler in your own apartment, we explained. She could reheat the spinach on the hot plate, making it much better than Room Service. We asked for lettuce and tomato salad. She was very proud of her vinaigrette dressing, which she had persuaded Father to adopt as the hotel's house dressing. She often said, "The trick is not to use good olive oil. I found that out years ago. Bessie, the cook who taught me how to make it, when I complained the first time I made it, she said, 'I bet you used good olive oil. You can't. You have to use Wesson.' Ever since then, it's been just the way you boys like it."

We asked for icebox cake, not the sort that Paul the Pastry Chef knew how to make. Instead, it was made with chocolate wafers standing on end and smothered with whipped cream. Left in the refrigerator overnight, it achieved a cakelike consistency, approaching magic. We considered it miraculous, even beyond the ethereal Jell-O whip Chef spun for us to improbable heights.

We'd agree on a night at least a month ahead. A week later she'd notice that the tomatoes hadn't been good recently. Maybe we should ask Brian at the Irish market. He used to save special slices of smoked salmon for Grandmother; he could watch out for some nice tomatoes for us.

"How about the meat?" Chef would grind some nice sirloin steaks for us, but we'd ask him to add a little ground round to keep the meat from getting too dry. "Who likes it rare?" "We both do." "If it's too rare, it's not good for you." "What about steak tartare?" we'd ask. "That's different."

Generally sometime during the third week, she'd change her mind. "I've got a lot to do," she'd say. "You boys think it's easy fixing dinner for you. You're all so fussy. You're spoiled. If you had to earn money to buy the shrimp and roast beef you put away every night, you wouldn't think it was so funny."

The fourth week she'd remember that Peter didn't like onion but forget whether I preferred it chopped in with the meat or would accept onion juice instead. The waiter could bring either on the side when he brought the ground meat. The point was that if the onion was chopped, she would have to mix the meat for Peter and me separately, but if she used onion juice, Peter wouldn't know the difference.

The day before the dinner, the waiter brought up a bowl of freshly whipped cream. She had already sent Robbins out for the chocolate cookies for the icebox cake. In the afternoon on the day of the dinner—"You boys didn't have hamburgers for lunch did you? What did you have? If you had hamburgers, my God, I could kill you"—the waiter would bring up a bowl holding three or four pounds of ground sirloin, decorated across the top with a grid shaped by the back of Chef's knife and circled with parsley. A second bowl held a head of iceberg lettuce leaves, separated and washed. There were whole tomatoes as well as a platter of tomato slices. The waiter would have forgotten the onion juice and be sent back down to the kitchen for it.

Father came upstairs at six-thirty, as usual. "Hello, boys. What's up? How about some nice roast beef tonight? Just the way you like it, rare. Maybe we ought to start with clam chowder. I saw Chef just now and he told me the chowder is wonderful."

"Stop that. Do you want to drive me out of my mind?" Mother would stand in the doorway of the tiny kitchen, waiting for the waiter to ring the doorbell again. He arrived with a room service table set with china and silver.

With eyes averted, praying he hadn't forgotten anything else, he tidied the place settings. As he left, he wished us a wonderful dinner.

"You don't want your hamburger too rare, do you?" she'd ask Father. "I'll make yours first. You boys will have to wait." She'd bring out his hamburger and look at him anxiously, waiting for him to take the first bite. Then she'd bring ours. She was too nervous to eat, herself. "Can you taste the onion?" she'd ask Peter. "You have to have a little. The meat doesn't taste like anything without it." "It's fine," he reassured her.

For days afterward, she would ask us how we *really* liked the dinner. The toaster-broiler was undependable. The hamburger had not been rare enough, not thick enough, too dry. Peter had tasted the onion. I hadn't. She'd throw questions at us unexpectedly, to trick us into telling the truth.

After graduating from Harvard—Mother turned out to be right about Harvard, after all—I returned home with a glass-and-walnut tobacco humidor and a set of beautiful briar pipes that Mother had bought and sent me a week or two after I started college. I rubbed them against my nose a lot to bring out the grain, but they burned my mouth and I didn't smoke them often. For Mother though, the pipes were nearly worth the tuition.

I had written a senior thesis on movies—all those afternoons in the theaters of Times Square had left me hopelessly addicted—and decided to make for myself a life in Cinema, preferably foreign Cinema. With subtitles. Someone at the hotel helped me get an entry-level job at MGM's New York office down the street. Admittedly, no subtitles, but real movies. On my first day, while I was forging Mario Lanza's autograph on eight-by-ten glossies, the manager of the department walked over to me. "We've been advertising for three weeks for a high-school graduate with no takers. Why are you here, for Christ's sake?" Without looking up from Lanza's pompadour, I said, "Connections."

Then I worked for a company that made TV commercials. I became a film critic for a small magazine. Not movies, film. Eyes moist over Ingrid Bergman or Barbara Stanwyck, I'd return to my small room at the Taft and write scathing reviews. My arcane analyses of simple-minded thrillers and melodramas, years before the French caught on to that particular scam, won me a following among a coterie of about twenty other film enthusiasts. My new friends argued over translations of Eisenstein's theories; they even argued over the translation of his movie titles—"Not *'Battleship' Potemkin, 'Light Destroyer' Potemkin,* for Christ sake."

In the company of chain-smoking biographers of D. W. Griffith and Edwin S. Porter, and pale critics who saw no films made after 1927, I spent my days in the film auditorium of the Museum of Modern Art. Leaving the museum one afternoon, I came across a girl I knew, crying her eyes out. *Orphans of the Storm* (Griffith. 1921. Billy Bitzer cameraman. Dorothy and Lillian Gish.) was pretty good but not worth those tears.

"What's wrong?"

"Seymour broke our engagement."

"What happened?"

"I couldn't find my purse and I missed the first reel." More sobs.

"Well, Seymour really loves *Orphans of the Storm*."

"I know, but it's the third time this week we've seen it."

None of my jobs paid enough for me to move out of the Taft. To give me some privacy, Father found me a room farther away, at the other end of the floor. Though I still could not steel myself to bring girls home late at night past assistant managers, room clerks, and elevator operators, I found girls who were willing to make love before dinner.

Sensing my drifting and dissatisfaction, thinking I needed still more privacy, perhaps hoping to wean me away from the hotel, Father found a small room for me on the roof, hardly part of the hotel at all. Taking the elevator as high as it would go, I'd walk down a hall, then climb a flight of stairs. I could walk out of my room, take three steps to a fire door, and be outside. New York had never seemed as beautiful as it did that year, 1953. The frenetic construction that took place in the sixties had not yet muddied the city's hard-etched skyline. I looked out over the lights of Manhattan to Central Park and Harlem beyond. I looked west across the ink-black Hudson to the New Jersey Palisades.

The next year, Peter and I both left the city. He married and found a job with the State Department. He was assigned to Taiwan, as far from the Taft as it was possible to be and still remain planet-bound. Deciding that graduate school was the only way out of my low-paying jobs, but not having yet figured out that those low-paying jobs were due to my arcane choice of career, I solved my problems by moving to Italy to study Cinema. (I saw the same movies, now without the subtitles.)

After two years, I returned from Italy, broke. Peter and his wife, Rachel, came back from Taiwan at about the same time, with a year-old son, Jacob. We all moved back into the hotel while we looked for work. Each evening we met with Mother and Father in 1588 for cocktails. The waiter brought meat and vegetables puréed by the sous-chef for the baby. We passed the dinner menu from hand to hand. Rachel was as horrified by the prices on the menu as Esther had been—more so because prices had tripled since the Depression. She wasn't hungry. "How about a broiled spring chicken?" Peter suggested. "That's light." She'd shake her head stubbornly.

Peter soon found work on Wall Street and moved his family into an apartment of their own. I managed to find a job with a distributor of Russian, Hungarian, and Czechoslovakian films—this at the height of the cold war —and so could still not yet afford to leave the hotel. Peter brought his family to dinner at least once a week, now with a new baby daughter. Jacob learned to speak, and he would sit on the sofa and listen attentively as Peter read the menu to him. "You like stewed peaches. How about a roast beef sandwich with Russian dressing and some nice stewed peaches?"

Finally finding a job in the audio-visual division of a large publishing company—one that did not verge on bankruptcy at the end of each month—I moved into an apartment of my own. Still, for as long as Mother and Father lived at the Taft, I signed for my food and drink there. Sometimes I ate upstairs with Mother and visited with Aunt Mick or other family friends, diving into those cold platters of turkey, ham, and roast beef, which ensured that Mother never lacked for company. Occasionally, I ate with Father in the Tap Room. It was difficult, though, for him to pay attention either to his lunch or to me. He was constantly aware of a waiter not at his station or someone being a nuisance at the bar.

Regularly, I had lunch with an old movie actor—a friend of Mother and Father's—who'd been a hit in a Broadway comedy in the thirties and had gone on to Hollywood. He'd appeared in a hundred movies as the reporter, the lawyer, a boss, a crook—a wise guy with a pencil mustache and a quirky eyebrow. People at nearby tables knew they had seen him before but couldn't remember where. If he wanted to, he'd do the thing with the quirky eyebrow, and they'd recognize him and come over and ask for an autograph. He had grown children but I think had lost touch. I was a great audience for his stories about his early days in stock and even vaudeville. Whenever Father walked through the Tap Room and saw us, he'd come over and say hello. I don't know if he envied the old actor my rapt attention.

Treating friends to sundaes and sodas in the Coffee Shop turned into treating them to martinis and manhattans in the Tap Room. It was a great place to take girls. When a blind date asked me once why the Taft instead of a dozen East Side restaurants she probably thought of as more elegant, I answered, without going into detail, "They know me there." As it happened, the doorman was new, the assistant manager was not in his glass cubicle, the bell captain didn't look up as we walked by. Neither Victor nor Mr. Stoler was on duty behind the Tap Room's glass door. We were seated at a table with a new waiter. It may have been a Sunday night when there were relief crews. Half-amused, half-suspicious, the girl asked, "What do you mean? Who knows you?"

"Everybody." Then I saw Father walking through the room, his hands clasped behind his back. I gave him a big wave, knowing he would not respond. His eyes flicked toward our table and he continued on.

"I suppose you know him, too," the girl said. "I certainly do." "Who is he?" "My father."

Sometimes, when I arrived at my office and finished my coffee and muffin, I'd pick up the phone and invite a girl to lunch at the Grill. We'd dance for an hour or two and then I'd return to work for the rest of the afternoon. I may have been more productive back at work than my more successful classmates, who had been filling up on cheap gin and paté in bad West Side French restaurants. I don't know what my bosses thought. Publishing's two-martini-lunch rule was still in force all over midtown; perhaps no one noticed how long I was gone.

Those were the days of the big bands. A couple in from Shaker Heights or Winnetka could go out dancing every evening of the week at a different hotel: Guy Lombardo was at the Roosevelt Grill, Jimmy Dorsey at the Pennsylvania, Chauncey Gray at the Ambassador, and Vincent Lopez at the Taft. Only Lopez played at lunch. He had played at the Taft for so many years he was rumored to own the hotel. A broadcast, *Luncheon with Lopez,* went out to the hinterlands. Women listened while making sandwiches and pouring milk for their children. Contests that Lopez interspersed throughout the broadcast, like "Shake the Maracas," must have sounded enticing enough, even over the radio, to make them want to come to the Grill when they visited New York. Father hoped they'd stay at the Taft.

The Grill was popular not only with tourists but also for office parties. Secretaries danced with each other at birthdays and engagements while their friends clapped and giggled. I remember entrees for less than two dollars, without a cover or minimum. The band broke often to give people a chance to eat their lunch before everything grew cold.

It wasn't hard to find girls willing to go dancing at lunch. In the fifties, long before dress-for-success and executive running shoes, there were some young women who, without embarrassment, didn't work and didn't want to. And more than a few trainees at Bloomie's or J. Walter Thompson were only marking time, waiting for marriage (though probably not with someone who had nothing better to do than go dancing at lunch).

When he saw me, the maitre d' would whisk us past the line already waiting to get in, saying loudly that my reserved table was ready. Embarrassed to walk past those waiting on line—I still thought of other adults as grownups—I lacked the confidence to ask the maitre d' to stop. Mr. Lopez would interrupt whatever he was playing, beam at the girl I happened to be with, and play "I'm in Love with a Wonderful Guy." During the band's frequent breaks, Mr. Lopez would stop at my table and fuss over me to impress my date. Again I was embarrassed, but I couldn't ask Lopez to stop any more than I could the maitre d'. Not that it would have mattered to him. Smooth and distracted, he seemed interested only in himself, probably not an unusual trait in bandleaders. A pianist, he gave us plaster casts of his hands one Christmas.

Holding a girl close in the middle of the day was very pleasant, particularly when sandwiched between the kinds of office chores a young man starting out late like me was likely to get. When I think of work then, I smell dusty files, yellow copy paper, and fluorescent lights. When I think of lunch, I smell Arpege, Tigresse, and Ma Griffe.

eight

After the war, New York smelled of money and possibility, the most attractive possibility being that of making more money. As the Taft made more, so did Father, although Mother was unhappy that he was so conservative. He wouldn't or couldn't *deal*. He refused invitations to invest in a new hotel, as owner-manager. He warned us all of a new depression. He had seen it in Germany; he had seen it in New York; he didn't want to be burned a third time. He stuck to the Taft like glue.

The Great Depression lasted just a dozen years, but it lingered on in ways that only those who lived through it can understand. Besides, he thought of money as the result of hard work, not speculation. He would not have appreciated the joke about the men who keep buying and selling a crate of herring, each time at a profit, until the last buyer opens a can of the stuff and tastes it. "This herring is awful!" he exclaims. "It's rancid!" "Of course," the man who sold it to him says. "It's not for eating; it's for buying and selling."

A hotel breaks even when three-quarters of its rooms are full. All our rooms were booked all the time. If the occupancy rate had been any higher, Father joked, the Taft would have been renting rooms twice a night, like its predecessor, the Manger. Permanent residents, like the little lady with the big hat and the Chihuahua, stayed on after the war, at rent-controlled rates, until the hotel offered them thousands of dollars to leave. The Taft was making so much money that the owners didn't begrudge a few thousand dollars to encourage the permanents on their way. Some permanents stayed on anyway, walking through the lobby and past the Coffee Shop through the thirties, forties, fifties, and sixties.

Though the Depression had knocked out whatever adventurous spirit Father might once have had, he was still the best hotelman in the city. He figured out ways to keep rooms profitable even when they were being painted. He assigned a crew to inspect rooms on a continuing basis. Those they identified as ready for repainting were earmarked for guests arriving late and were painted early in the day. Other hotels lost rooms for two or three days when they were painted, and so they delayed maintenance—it cost too much lost revenue.

Father should have been happier, but the business was changing. As labor costs rose, he agonized for months before switching from elevator operators to push-button cars. As transatlantic steamships and transcontinental trains disappeared, so did the heavy trunks that had accompanied the passengers. There was little need for porters in addition to bellmen.

The Civil Rights Act made it against the law to hire only black bellmen. Alfred thought the bellmen looked terrific —if he could have, he would have hired them all in the same shade of brown. A deep need for order is part of the hotel trade. Departments were organized by race or nationality. If the chef was French, the sous-chef was French. Martin the Porter hired the sons of cousins and acquaintances or boys recommended by people he knew or who knew people he knew, from the same county he came from in Ireland. People taking care of their own has a cozy sound, unless, of course, their own doesn't include you. Father approved of the system, even though he would not have been hired by the Irish-dominated hotels of the time.

"The next thing they'll do is integrate the Gae Foster Girls," he said. "Can you think of anything dumber than a pair of black legs in the middle of that chorus line?"

"They have blondes and brunettes and no one cares," I pointed out.

"Oh, for Christ's sakes, that's the dumbest argument I've ever heard!"

The next week I told him (with some sense of triumph) that I had read that the Roxy was being sued by the Civil Rights Commission because of their segregated chorus line. "That's the dumbest thing I've ever heard!"

A left-wing organization picketed a film at the Roxy, and a Seventh Avenue doorman spotted a Taft waiter marching. He complained to the personnel office, who told him it was none of his business. He went to Walter Winchell, who visited the Taft barbershop every evening for a shave. Winchell put an item in his column about the commie waiter; Father fired the doorman. The doorman went to Ed Sullivan, another tabloid columnist, who also had a popular television show. Within twenty-four hours, the Catholic War Veterans were picketing the Taft. Every day in his column, Sullivan wrote about the doorman, a war veteran fired for anticommunism while reds continued to serve unsuspecting Americans at the Taft. Father stopped watching *The Ed Sullivan Show*.

He was nearly seventy, had run the hotel his way for thirty years, and now he had to hire white bellmen, lose black elevator operators entirely, worry about how long he could keep his Irish porters, and listen to civil rights commissions and gossip columnists tell him how to run his hotel. But these annoyances were trivial compared with the problems success brought the Taft.

Bursting with cash, the hotel wafted the irresistible pheromone of money for miles. In the mid-fifties, an investor bought the hotel at a price so high it made Father shake his head. He worried that in order for the new owner to show a profit on his investment, he'd have to cut back on maintenance. Instead, the owner spent $2 million air-conditioning the hotel and installing TV. Within a year, he sold the Taft to another investor for a sum that made Father shake his head still harder. Mother wanted Father to invest his own money with the second owner, but he refused. He thought the new owner had paid too much. He hadn't foreseen that the second new owner would quickly sell the hotel to a third new owner, for more money than Father or anyone else, including the first new owner, could have imagined.

Ultimately, Father's concern about the high price investors were willing to pay for the hotel turned out to be correct. New Owner Number Three, who had bought many hotels but always sold them before he had time to learn the hotel business, explained to Father that he could not afford to pay bills on time. Everything depended on float—the use of other people's money for as long as possible. Other people in this case included the butcher, the fish wholesaler, the bakeries that brought bread each morning. Father's system of paying bills the day after they were received, rather than at the end of the month, had ensured that he got the best beef and lamb and pork. But after a year of slow pay, the butcher refused to leave meat without being paid in cash, which he carefully counted before leaving. The meat the Taft got was whatever the butcher's other customers did not want. When Father explained that to the owner, he explained float to Father all over again.

Mother pointed out that all the new owners had been successful. New Owner Number Three, by using what he called float (the butcher called it "*my* money, the cheap bastard"), bought the Roxy next door and sold it to investors. He also sold them the air rights over the theater, which belonged to the Taft. The investors tore the Roxy down and raised a forty-story office building against the windows of our most expensive suites, turning them as dark as the cheapest rooms facing the air shafts. Those windows were bricked in, and Mother bought expensive Chinese scenic wallpaper with sages and pagodas and bridges to paste on the new living room wall. As hard as Father thought about profit, it had never occurred to him to sell our air.

The owner sold the Coffee Shop to a chain of cheap restaurants. Father came upstairs after a meeting with the men who had bought it. They specialized in restaurants on high traffic corners, they told him, because they needed the kind of traffic you can only get on busy corners. No one ate at their places twice, they explained. The food wasn't good and cost too much.

"Don't be silly, Alfred. They were joking," Mother said, but she soon found out they weren't.

Other hotels offered him jobs, but he was unwilling to make his rounds half a dozen times a day in some other lobby. He became ill and went into the hospital—the doctors thought it was an inflammation of the heart wall, but the infection didn't respond to antibiotics. The doctors were puzzled. He didn't get better, and he didn't die. He finally returned to the hotel weak and still sick. He went downstairs each day, at least for a few hours. The whole hotel thought he was dying. We could see it in the faces of the maids and the room service waiters. Everyone spoke to him very gently.

There was no reason not to retire. Peter, his wife, and now three young children lived in a sunny apartment overlooking the Hudson. I had accepted a job in Chicago and was getting ready to move there. Father and Mother moved to Florida. It didn't take long to clear out our four rooms.

nine

After Mother and Father left the hotel, they moved into a condominium in Florida. He gradually got better. For a few years, they came to New York in the summer, staying at a residential East Side hotel in the seventies. Mother said Father avoided the Taft, just as he had the Knickerbocker. For some years they continued to go to Europe, staying at four-star hotels and visiting with the managers there. Mother noted with surprise that she usually caught a cold or the flu shortly after arriving in Rome or Paris or Lake Como. "It's so annoying," she said. "There we are in Europe and I'm in bed looking at a room service table. I might as well be home!"

As they got older, Mother rarely left their refrigerated condominium. Though for thirty years they had been the focus of bellmen, waiters, maids, cashiers, and pastry chefs, they didn't seem to miss it. Mother no longer fussed about food or sent anything back. Father took a walk each afternoon to buy a steak or a take-out roast chicken. When Peter or I came down to Florida to visit, Mother would tell Father to take us to the pool. "The exercise will do you good."

Years later, when Mother was dying, at dusk she'd search restlessly for a phone, knocking over water glasses and boxes of tissue on the bedside table. "It's dinnertime," she'd say. "Who's ready for a drink?" She'd look up at the nurse. "Who are you? Are you staying for dinner? What would you like? Are the boys here?" She'd turn and look at us. "What are you going to have? Where are the menus?"

Mother and Father had been living in Florida for five years when I checked into the Taft with my new family, my first time back since we had all left the Taft in 1968. In those five years, I had moved to Chicago to run the media program for a bright young educational publishing company recently acquired by IBM. I had finally gotten serious about work and had been promoted to run the elementary school division, the most profitable part of the company. I managed about sixty editors and was living in a Mies van der Rohe building overlooking the lake when I fell in love with Nancy, a young widow with two preteen daughters.

This was our first trip together. Visiting the Taft was the culmination of a vacation that had begun in Washington, D.C. On the plane, my new daughters, Lisa and Jenny, had eaten all the peanuts they could cadge from the stewardesses. Leaning across the aisle, I smiled insincerely and said, "We've got a real nice dinner planned for tonight. If you keep on eating those peanuts, you won't want any dinner." They smiled vacantly at me, as if I were an in-flight movie, and kept eating peanuts. That evening, in Washington, they didn't want dinner. Persuading Nancy that they were old enough to be left alone for a few hours (Lisa was thirteen, Jenny nine), I told them what fun room service was and how to order sandwiches if they were hungry.

At the restaurant, while we waited for cocktails, the captain came up to me. "There's a call. It's a young girl." Nancy bolted from the table. "It's nothing," I said, following close behind. She let me pick up the phone, too frightened to speak.

"Stephen." It was Lisa. "There's a fire in the hotel."

Nancy punched me in the arm, her eyes wide. "Where are you?" I asked.

"We're in the lobby. In our pajamas. We walked down the stairs." The reproach in her voice was overwhelming. "There are lots of grownups here. They're in their pajamas, too." Nancy sat silent in the cab on the way back to the hotel. Then: "We're not going to leave them alone again." "I know," I said.

The girls were sitting on a sofa facing the lobby entrance in their slippers and pajamas. "You shouldn't have left us alone," Jenny said. "I know," I said. When, finally, the firemen decided it had been a false alarm, we took the elevator back upstairs and ordered ice cream.

The next day, President Eisenhower died and all the government monuments and museums closed. The girls' relief was palpable. They closeted themselves with Nancy for five minutes, then suggested that we spend the rest of the week at Bergdorf's and Bonwit's and Saks Fifth Avenue in New York. We could stay at the Taft.

I called to ask Father to reserve our apartment, if he could. Mother wanted to speak to the girls. Lisa told her about the hotel fire, and then Mother wanted to speak to me. "It was a false alarm," I said.

"You shouldn't have left them alone," she said. "I know."

When we arrived at the Taft, the whole hotel knew we were coming. Father had reserved our apartment on the fifteenth floor. Bellmen quickly surrounded us. The girls seemed stunned over the fuss everyone made over me, and them. "They look just like you," one bellman said. "Look how they've grown," said another. The girls looked at me first inquiringly, then puzzled, as they realized I wasn't going to explain to these uniformed men that they had never seen the girls before in their lives.

Someone asked about Father and Mother. Someone else said Mr. Russo in the front office had received a postcard from Father and taped it on the wall for everyone to read. A bellman, deciding it was time to move on, took our bags. The elevators had been push-button automatic for many years, so I could not show Lisa and Jenny how to play Elevator Free-Fall. Just as well. As we walked down the long corridor to our suite, the bellman asked about Peter. When I told him that Peter had two boys and two little girls, he shook his head and said, "My, my."

Our door at the end of the hall no longer said 1586-1589; now, painted gilt letters read "The Lewis Suite." The girls were very impressed; so was I. Reaching into my pocket for a tip caused the bellman to shake his head. "Oh, no." "Come on," I put the money in his hand. "Do you still call them Bathroom Charlies?" I asked. (Bathroom Charlies head for the toilet as soon as they get in their rooms. They flush and wash their hands until the bellman gives up and leaves without a tip.)

After he left, Lisa asked about the lies they had heard in the lobby: that she and Jenny looked like me and how much they had grown. Everyone had been delighted to see me, I explained, happy to see my wife and children. But people who work for tips make themselves agreeable without stopping to think about it, like your leg jerking when the doctor hits your knee with a hammer. They were talking about us even now. I told the girls about Smitty the Waiter, who with the help of a napkin bunny and brassiere, had retired to a country home bought with fifty years of tips. He couldn't have done that if he had followed their dictum of sincerity and truth in all things.

Leading the way through the suite, I showed my wife and daughters how little space we had actually needed to make a family home. "Here's where my grandmother lived. Here's where Peter and I grew up. I used to creep out of my bed and grab his foot when he was asleep. This was the living room. That wallpaper of the Chinese man fishing is where there used to be a window. Peter and I would peek at the chorus girls sunbathing on the Roxy roof down below. A chorus girl is a kind of dancer." Mother's bedroom still smelled of her, I thought, a fainter version of her purse—perfume and cigarettes and gumdrops and chocolate and lavender smelling salts.

I was nearly forty when we married. Nancy lived in a Victorian house on the corner of a well-to-do street in a well-to-do suburb of Chicago. I moved in. About family life, I was what theologians call invincibly ignorant: never having had a chance to know the truth, I could not be blamed for my shortcomings. Saved from Hell but sentenced to Limbo. Exploring our mazy basement one afternoon, I came upstairs to tell Nancy, "There's dozens of extra windows down there. Why don't you get rid of them?" I assumed that they were left over from one of the many remodelings that had been undertaken over the past century. When she explained that they were storm windows, my heart sank. Dubious about my permanent stay in the suburbs, I now knew with certainty that I could look forward to a life of incompetence and continual humiliation. "Are you crazy?" I yelled in exasperation. "There's no way for me to get all those up in time before a storm!"

Marrying a widow with children is entering the family drama at intermission. There's no way to change Act One or even to be sure what has actually happened. The culture I was so anxious to transmit to my new offspring wasn't of much use in the suburbs. I was able to teach Lisa and Jenny little but what Father had taught me. Learning to take the swizzle stick out of your drink so that you won't poke yourself in the eye with it was of little use to them, and that only much later. "Always walk away from the buildings and close to the street," I cautioned my daughters, worried that muggers could dart out from a doorway, sprint across twenty yards of manicured lawn, and harm these soft and pretty charges who had been put into my keeping. (After a while, I grew more realistic and started worrying about alcohol, pot, and good-looking, clean-cut boys.) Still, after a few years, the girls were ordering *escargots* and *lapin à la moutarde* while their friends still thought that Swiss instead of American cheese on their hamburgers was pushing the envelope. When Jenny, as a birthday present, asked for dinner at Le Français, recently voted one of the best restaurants in America, I beamed with fatherly delight.

$\mathcal{T}$he next time I visited the Taft was on a trip to New York in the seventies. After lunch with a friend, we took a leisurely walk up Forty-second Street. Stan's work was going poorly. Rather than return to his office to frustrated subordinates and problems he couldn't solve, he took the afternoon off.

We passed the Forty-second Street theaters of my childhood, awaiting, as they had for years, grandiose plans for renewal. "All Nude" placards were in front of what had once been Hubert's Dime Museum, where Professor Roy Heckler put fleas through their paces, pulling chariots, turning miniature carousels, and occasionally dining on his arm. I told Stan about the Great Waldo, who swallowed mice, and Sailor White, the strongman who lifted weights attached to rings through his nipples. I had watched, fascinated, not so much by the feat of strength as by his pendulous breasts—as close as I could get at the time to seeing breasts not my mother's.

We passed a fast-food franchise that had replaced Grants, a giant Forty-second Street saloon with the best hot dogs and the cheapest whisky in the city. A policeman on the corner heard me describing the place to Stan and broke in. "That place was rough." He turned to the policeman standing with him. "Remember Grants, Harry?" Harry didn't. The first cop said, "We was scared to go in." I hadn't known that. Grants had been my favorite stop after a Laff Movie. Probably still tranced out after two or three hours of two-reel comedies, I was oblivious to the lowlifes standing shoulder to shoulder around me.

The cop tossed me a friendly gesture, halfway between a wave and a salute, and said, in the tone one old veteran uses to another, "It sure has changed here." It sure had. Two little boys playing in Times Square now would be lucky to meet nothing worse than the relatively good-hearted, slow-moving Frankenstein who had scared us out of our movie seats forty years before.

The signs and billboards of my childhood were gone. The Maxwell House coffee cup, endlessly pouring, had run dry. Little Lulu, ceaselessly pulling Kleenex, had given up. Johnny Walker, "since 1820 and still going strong," was no longer going strong; was, in fact, gone. The Camels billboard's painted smoker, after twenty-five years of chain-smoking, looked it. The movie palaces, too, all gone. The nightclubs of my youth—Club Zanzibar, the Latin Quarter, Billy Rose's Diamond Horseshoe, the French Casino, and more—long gone. Even the taxi dance halls—the Orpheum Dance Palace, Parisian Dance Land, Honeymoon

Lane, the Tango Dance Palace—had proven unable to compete with live sex shows.

"Come on," I said to Stan, as we passed the Taft, "I'll show you where I grew up." He held back. "Are you sure?" I saw what he meant. The hotel was in the terminal stages of neglect. The Seventh Avenue entrance to the Grill was boarded up. The lobby's swinging double doors were bolted shut; the revolving doors too grimy to see through. "Come on," I said. "This may be your last chance before it falls down."

By then the Taft was one of the cheapest hotels in the city. "All you can stay for twenty-five dollars," I joked to Peter. New Owner Number Three had long since gone bankrupt. So had New Owners Four and Five. The week before, according to a cab driver, someone had jumped or been thrown, naked, out of an upper floor window.

Stan and I walked through the empty lobby, the sofas and chairs gone—sold or seized by a creditor. The one clerk behind the registration desk dozed, his head on his arms on the marble counter. He didn't—or couldn't—look up as Stan followed me to the marble steps leading down to the Grill. Through the dirty Grill Room doors, I saw chairs upended on the tables. The Grill had been rented out to a steakhouse chain; finally, even they had given up. I pushed open a heavy brass door, unmarked, that led to the kitchen and pantries. From the dark, a large black man with a stick in his fist challenged us. "What are you doing here?" "My father was manager here a long time ago," I said nervously. He walked close and looked me over. "You Mr. Lewis' boy?" To my surprise, my eyes filled with tears. I nodded. "We was just talking about him. He's gone now, right?"

I said he had died a few years before.

"How's your mom?"

"She's fine. In Florida."

He nodded. "You remember Margaret the Housekeeper? She passed just last year." We talked about her and her husband, Jack the Porter, and a few employees still in the neighborhood. He asked about Peter. I said we talked two or three times a week and that he was fine. As I said goodbye, he waved his stick at the shadows around us. "Sure glad your father never had to see this." But he had, of course. He was such a good hotelman he had seen it from the day New Owner Number Three sold the Coffee Shop, maybe from the day the hotel was bought by New Owner Number One, to be sold like the herring in the old, unfunny joke.

The last time I visited the Taft, it was being gutted in preparation for its transformation into a short-lived hotel that was eventually replaced by the Michelangelo. I called the developer and improvised a semifiction about learning to read seated on the toilet, in front of the printed tiles in our bathroom. I asked if I could have a few tiles as a souvenir. He invited me to take a look at the work going on at the hotel, gave me the name of the foreman, and told me to take as many tiles as I wanted. And how about the bronze lions' heads at the ends of the bannisters leading to the Grill? I wanted to know, thinking quickly. Did he know those? He certainly did, he said, and he was keeping them for himself.

The sidewalk in front of the Taft was blocked by giant dumpsters filled with broken slabs of marble and thick chunks of masonry. Clouds of cement dust drifted out from the bronze doors. Inside, bare bulbs hung from the gilt ceiling, though the chandelier was still in place. The marble balustrade around the mezzanine was already gone. Even the greasy spoon that had replaced the Coffee Shop was temporarily boarded over. Plywood offices for foremen and engineers were scattered about the lobby. I introduced myself to the foreman, a few years younger than I.

"You lived here?" he asked. "Gee. I grew up on Tenth Avenue. What a mess this town is now. You still live here?"

"No."

"Lucky."

The steps to the Grill were blocked, but he sent one of his men with me to the Tap Room. The horseshoe bar had been ripped out and so had the wall behind it. The Tap Room, the Village Room, and a separate kitchen for the Tap Room were now one vast space. The fake Spanish balconies and plaster vines in the Village were hanging off the walls. I could see where the original owners had attached their annex to the original hotel, an event which in my childhood had seemed to date back into the mists of pre-Arthurian times. The bronze-door elevators were still in good condition.

A few permanent tenants, who had kept their rent-controlled apartments despite my father's blandishments, now refused to leave for less than one hundred thousand dollars or so. The developers decided to keep the elevators running, provide the recalcitrants with electric heaters, and build around them. They gave each a safety helmet so they could walk through the lobby, hoping, I'm sure, that they would choke on the cement dust.

Workers were dismantling the fifteenth floor and I couldn't go there, but one of the men took me to other floors. Visiting gutted rooms doesn't take long, no matter how long you lived in them. I spent the last ten minutes of my half-hour tour wondering when I could ask to return to the lobby. The bathroom tiles were already wrapped in brown paper. "There aren't very many," the foreman apologized. "Is that OK?" I said it was fine. "A lot of them got broken when we were working on the bathrooms. These were the only good ones I could find." I said it was more than I'd expected and thanked him again. "In the old days I bet this was something," he said.

Peter had been too busy to join me, or perhaps didn't want to see the gutted ruin of the hotel, but we met for lunch. A partner in a successful investment bank, he took me to his dining club in the Rainbow Room on top of Rockefeller Center. We talked about the Taft, as we always did when we met. I gave him half the tiles and carried the rest home with me. The tiles are three by six inches, easy to carry as we have moved from house to house. I have six in a drawer in my bathroom right now. Three say PLEASE PLACE CURTAIN INSIDE TUB WHEN USING SHOWER, and the other three say PLEASE DO NOT THROW ANYTHING IN TOILET WHICH CAN CAUSE OVERFLOW OR DAMAGE.

On my next visit, the Taft is no longer the Taft; it has become the Michelangelo. Coming down to the lobby from my comped suite, I find a message waiting for me from the new manager, who would like to show me his hotel. His office is on the mezzanine, at the opposite end from Father's. Most of the mezzanine is gone, but there are stairs leading to a great open area, intended for meetings I suppose. Across from the elevators, there had been a writing area filled with desks, stationery, and scratchy pens and inkwells. To the left, there had been a bank of pay toilets. I realize the manager's offices are in the old personnel department, where Miss Hirsch once found jobs for me. Hoping that this is not a nightmare and I will not find Miss Hirsch inside with another terrible job waiting, I walk in. The office looks much the same; fair employment practice notices in English and Spanish are on the walls. I announce myself to the receptionist, and an attractive young woman comes out. She is the director of guest relations. Unfortunately, something has come up; the manager is occupied just now but will be delighted to have drinks with me at five. In the meantime, would I like her to show me around the back of the house? Is there anything I would particularly like to see? I recognize her, of course. She takes care of lost room reservations, complaints about drunks, and roaches in the bathroom. She is an assistant manager.

I'd like to go up on the roof, where Peter and I played a half century before. Unfortunately, the roof is part of the condominium next door.

Then the Grill. She doesn't think that will be possible just now; the Grill hasn't yet been remodeled.

"Then the kitchens."

In the basement, what had been Charlie's pantry is now a laundry room. Paul's pastry kitchen is an employee cafeteria. Workers eating lunch look up briefly, then turn back to their food. Father hated it when strangers—a supplier or a friend of one of the owners—walked alone through the back of the house, especially the kitchens. He said that unannounced visits always started rumors that the hotel had been sold. I don't think I look like someone in the market for a hotel; at least the workers don't seem concerned. But hotel workers learn to keep poker faces no matter what they see.

The new kitchens are only a small part of the original Taft kitchens, but they are big enough. The Italian restaurant upstairs is pricy—an embarrassed word that New Yorkers use when they are reluctant to admit that something is too expensive for them—and elite. Its menu would have been unintelligible to anyone eating in the Grill—tortellini, orechiette, and cannelloni might as well have been towns in Sicily. Spider crabs would have been anyone's guess.

There was little besides the kitchens and the Grill that I wanted to see. Our life at the Taft had revolved around food. The Depression constantly played in Father's head like some sinister background music, and he reminded us often of how much we would have had to pay for the food that we were served free.

Food is the first gift, after life itself, and it shouldn't be hard to understand its magic. When someone learns where and how I grew up, their first question is always "Could you have all the ice cream you wanted?" At a party in the suburbs, a man across the table told me that adventuring around the world twenty years before, he had met another American at a Bedouin banquet. Though the man's face seemed familiar, neither could place the other. As they sat on carpeted sand, their faces greasy with roast lamb, they exchanged information about schools, careers, and acquaintances without striking gold, until the other American mentioned that he had grown up at the Taft. The man told me he immediately exclaimed, "You were the one with the free milkshakes!" He had met Peter.

I'm told that once, under the fifty-foot Taft sign on the roof, I waved my cap over my head and shouted, "Three cheers for chocolate eclairs and hooray for Boston cream pie."

In *The Seven Storey Mountain,* Tom Merton said Bob Lax "was living in the Hotel Taft, tutoring the children of the manager, and having access to an icebox full of cold chicken at all hours of the day and night." If a potential saint, in a spiritual autobiography compared by Archbishop Fulton Sheen to *The Confessions of Saint Augustine,* finds free chicken worth mentioning, I suppose I shouldn't be too hard on myself.

The director of guest relations and I return to the mezzanine. She tells me about the new conference rooms, which are wired for overhead projectors, sixteen-millimeter film, and videotape. She points out that the Italian restaurant downstairs can cater. Having been to too many business meetings myself, I understand. Executives will be able to analyze the competition's successes and make excuses for their own declining sales while eating lunch—and ripping up their digestive tracts. If the Taft Grill never offered Adriatic spider crabs (if we had, we certainly never would have called them that), at least businessmen then could forget their worries for a while and dance with their girlfriends or teach their daughters to waltz.

Guest Relations reminds me that I am meeting the manager for cocktails later that afternoon, flashes me a guest relations smile, and slips back into her office. Peter and I rarely visited this end of the mezzanine. In the lobby, guests shared the excitement of Times Square; those few who, instead, were drawn to the mezzanine came for the solitude, the last thing Peter and I needed.

Elevator operators, exclusively black in the transparently racist days before the Second World War, used to call out, "Mezzaline, please" when they let passengers off there.

Father explained to me that black people, through some idiosyncrasy of soft palate or vocal cord, couldn't pronounce "mezzanine." No matter how we question and challenge our parents' opinions, their facts often slip past our guard, planting misinformation in our brains. It was years before I had any occasion to think about *mezzaline* again. When I did, I realized that, of course, a starter had gotten it wrong and trained the operators to mispronounce it, too.

We visited the mezzanine twice a year to have Dr. Kauffman, the chiropodist, check our feet. Though our soft children's feet couldn't have required much attention, I suppose we went because he didn't charge. He examined our soles and dug under our toenails—it was like a visit to the dentist, less painful, but more embarrassing. We also visited the house doctor, a stunned refugee from Yugoslavia who received his tiny office rent-free in exchange for his availability in the case of guest emergencies. He also treated his fellow Yugoslavs. For years, whenever I met someone from Yugoslavia, he invariably knew Dr. Kaufer.

He took care of Grandma Esther during her final illness, a series of small strokes and heart attacks. Mother would call him whenever Esther's breathing became labored or she put her hand up to her chest. He arrived at the apartment door within seconds. Once, when he could not be found immediately—he might have been having lunch or going to the bathroom—Mother, frantic with concern, screamed at him unmercifully.

I go downstairs to the Italian restaurant where the mail desk should be. It's packed with businessmen; I may be the only one there not on an expense account. Without a reservation, I am quickly taken to a terrific table—I am sure because of my escorted tour of the kitchens. Nothing's faster than the hotel telegraph. The maitre d' talks to me as if we had gone to school together, trying to find out if he's supposed to know me, wondering who the hell I am. For the first time ever, I spend my own money under this roof. The check I pay would have bought lunch in the Coffee Shop through the winter and spring of 1939. I hear Father speaking again, as he did when he signed our restaurant checks with what I used to call the magic words—Alfred Lewis—"Do you boys know what this would cost if you were paying for this yourselves?" I do now, Pop.

After lunch, out for a walk in the old neighborhood, I see that the Going Out of Business gift shop on the corner is gone. Though not its real name, "Going Out of Business" was all we ever called it, its windows permanently plastered with notices of a final, apocalyptic sale. As a child I had coveted the plaster Balinese profiles in bas relief, the fake Apfenzell lace, and the bisque figurines revolving on top of music boxes. That a stake has finally been driven through the heart of the Going Out of Business store convinces me that the West Side will prosper.

Across the street, the new Equitable Center dwarfs the Michelangelo. Expensive restaurants surround a courtyard that cuts through to Fifty-second Street. Giant, jaunty bronze hares by the English sculptor Barry Flanagan stand sentry at each end. A branch of the Whitney Museum is in the lobby. The possibility that the Equitable will anchor a classy, vital, expensive, *new* West Side has persuaded moneyed men to buy and gut the Taft. We're lucky. Other hotels, some far more elegant than ours—the old Ritz-Carlton and the Ambassador, with deluxe service that can't be matched by mini-bottles of shampoo—are gone. The Martinique, cousin to the Plaza and designed by the same architect, is a welfare flophouse.

As I look south toward Times Square, I see that office towers have begun to replace the shabby four-story buildings that supported the flashing signs of the Great White Way. In the sixties, the city eased the restrictions on size and land use in midtown. They hoped fewer restrictions, which meant greater potential for profit, would encourage developers to put their money into the West Side. When the developers held onto their land to make not just a killing but a slaughter, the city wised up and attached a deadline to the giveaway. Impelled by sunset provisions, office buildings shot up like flowers in a time-lapse movie. The little that is left, like the empty block I spotted from my fifth-floor suite, won't be vacant long. Bulldozers and cranes will soon hammer another sixty-story nail in Times Square's coffin. The Disneyfication of Times Square is still a few years in the future, but the city's requirement that the new office towers maintain the lights that signify Times Square to out-of-towners tells me that the city will preserve Times Square the way taxidermists preserve pet cats.

Times Square has a checkered history, none of it very good. John Jacob Astor bought the land around the village of Great Kill in 1803. William Vanderbilt bought it from him and put up the American Horse Exchange, a center of stables, a morass of mud and manure. In the 1890s, when theatrical entrepreneur Oscar Hammerstein, the songwriter's uncle, built the first theaters north of Forty-second Street, he had to bring in electricity. The neighborhood was then Longacre Square, though everyone called it Thieve's Lair. It didn't become Times Square until 1905, when the subway went in and the *New York Times* pressured the city to name the subway station under its presses after the paper.

Hammerstein's theaters generated more theaters, then restaurants and nightclubs. The hotel boom in the twenties added dozens of new hotels, including ours. But what seemed to be a new day was just another false dawn.

Soon, Prohibition killed first the nightclubs and then the restaurants, which depended on liquor sales. The Depression turned the theaters into cheap movie houses. The movies changed into burlesque houses, and the burlesque houses into live sex shows, where men paid a dollar for fifteen seconds to stand in darkened private booths and watch women offer gynecological displays.

On the corner of Fiftieth Street, a Roy Rogers Family Restaurant and a bar named TGIF—it stands for "Thank God It's Friday" and so is wrong six days out of seven—have replaced the Roxy box offices and lobby. The bar is on the second floor, either borrowed from the old Taft mezzanine or part of the loge level of the Roxy lobby. There are no customers—who'd climb a flight of stairs for a drink in Times Square? A bored bartender and a lethargic cashier let me wander. In the back, dishwashers eye me suspiciously. I look resentfully back at them. I think they may be in Father's office.

Returning to the Michelangelo for my meeting with the manager, I spot an unmarked fire door next to the concierge's desk. I wait until the concierge steps away and the desk clerk goes into a back room. Then I push it open. Sure enough, I face the wide sweep of stairs that led to the Grill. Holes along the marble wall show where the banisters have been pried out. Halfway down, at the turn of the stairs, the way is blocked by a heavy iron door. I know it is locked but I try it anyway. It's locked. Still, these stairs are all I've seen that hasn't been torn down or fixed up. As I peer closer at the grimy marble steps, the past and present conjoin. The edge of each step is rounded, smoothed by more than fifty years of footsteps, including mine. I'd like to touch one, but they're filthy. I straighten up and go out to the empty cocktail lounge.

It is not hard to spot the manager as he nears the cocktail area. Like Father, he *notices.* As he walks toward me, beginning to smile, getting ready to put out his hand, he is checking the lobby from the sides of his eyes. The bellman stands a little straighter, the room clerk at the registration desk busies himself with paperwork, the bartender, who had been gazing abstractedly at the wall, senses a change in the room, turns around, and starts polishing a glass.

This man who greets me is young and speaks with a very slight German accent. Father would be pleased; he felt that only the Swiss and the Germans shared his obsession with detail. The manager has come to New York from a hotel in Dallas, initially to open a different West Side hotel, which was owned by a Swedish consortium, which quickly sold it at a profit to the Japanese. The manager tells me proudly that all his 170 employees are signed up for Italian lessons. I hope they don't have to switch to Farsi soon to please a new group of owners.

The Italians paid $42 million for the Michelangelo's 178 rooms. The manager tells me it is a good price, one at which the new owners can make money. I hope so. The lobby we're in was built during the city's previous hotel boom, in the mid-1920s, which lasted up to the crash of '29—the papers for the Waldorf-Astoria, four blocks east, were signed the day before Black Friday (though it would be insensitive to bring this up now).

I ask what he intends to do with the Grill. He is not quite sure yet; perhaps a private dining room. It is difficult, he says, to know how to handle a basement dining room. He asks about the large space to the east of the current lobby; I tell him about the Tap Room and the Village. I ask about the Roy Rogers Family Restaurant and TGIF on the corner, marring the Michelangelo's façade (and taking the entire block down a couple of notches). His face clouds momentarily, but he brightens as he tells me about his bathrooms and bedrooms, the largest in the city. The Michelangelo is designed for upscale business travelers.

He details for me his plans for voice mail, modems, and fax machines in all the rooms, while I gnaw the Taft like an old dog with an old white bone, flesh gone, gristle gone, taste gone, smell gone, only memory urging him on.

Revolving doors half a dozen feet behind me once circled constantly as pedestrians broke ranks on Seventh Avenue and entered. Bellmen stationed inside pushed on the bronze frames of the revolving doors and started them moving as soon as anyone approached. The swinging doors on the sides hung in double sets with space between to trap hot summer or cold winter air before it could enter the lobby along with the trunks and suitcases that flowed to and from the street. Lines of check-ins stood in front of the registration clerks. Checkouts waited for their bills at the cashiers' cages. Clerks called out, "Front." Bellmen paged guests. Tourists sent telegrams, bought newspapers and theater tickets and tiny souvenir Empire State Buildings. They waited for elevators. They had their shoes shined. They rose from sofas and chairs to shake hands with friends, greeted lunch dates in front of the Coffee Shop or the Tap Room. They stared up at people leaning over the mezzanine balustrade, who in turn stared down at them. When I came down from the fifteenth floor and the elevator doors opened onto the mezzanine to let guests on or off, a sound like a rushing waterfall rose to meet me —a hundred voices talking all at once, an excited sound that anticipated the eddies of the crowded lobby below, alive with a multitude of strangers whom, in a moment— "Lobby, please. Getting out, please. Lobby, please"— I would join.

CPSIA information can be obtained
at www.ICGtesting.com
Printed in the USA
LVHW03s2230130918
590104LV00002B/2/P